HOW JESUS
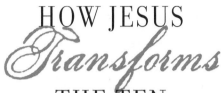
Transforms
THE TEN
COMMANDMENTS

by
EDMUND P. CLOWNEY
with
REBECCA CLOWNEY JONES

P&R
PUBLISHING
P.O. BOX 817 • PHILLIPSBURG • NEW JERSEY 08865-0817

CONTENTS

FOREWORD

This book, like all my father's work, was born of his passion for the church and for Jesus, the Lord of the church. This particular volume began as a series of adult Sunday school lessons at Christ the King Presbyterian Church in Houston, Texas, where my father accepted a two-year, full-time position as associate pastor at the age of 82. At the time, he was writing a longer volume on another subject entirely, but the needs of the church took precedence and he began the series on the Ten Commandments. Both projects moved along slowly, and as time took its toll on my father's energy and concentration, it became apparent that he should finish the shorter work before turning his attention to the longer.

In 2002, my parents moved to Charlottesville, Virginia, where my father took up an honorary post as theologian in residence at Trinity Presbyterian Church, a church he had served in a similar position from 1984 to 1990. When I visited my parents, my father and I always discussed his writing projects. His "write tight" style had gotten a little too tight, and he asked me to aerate this text, to smooth out transitions and to add some illustrations. In November 2004, we worked together to flesh out some of the shorter chapters, using the notes from his Sunday school lessons. I took the manuscript back to California, leaving my dad free to work on the longer book. When I finished the changes and additions, I sent it to him for approval. My editorial touch is more present in this book than it was in the one or two others he asked me to look over. However, my father read and approved all changes to the manuscript and in early February, 2005, I sent the files to the publisher.

On February 26, while getting up to help my mother with the Saturday vacuuming, my father fell and broke his sacrum. During his consequent hospitalization, complications arose that eventually overwhelmed him. On March 8, the same day I flew from California to be with my parents, I received e-mail confirmation that the manuscript had been accepted for publication. That evening, when I arrived at the University of Virginia hospital, I gave my dad the good news. His face brightened and he gave me a thumbs-up sign. "Dad," I said, "you've got to get well now so you can sign the contract." But it was his wife of 63 years, Jean Clowney, who signed the contract. On Palm Sunday (March 20, 2005, at 6:30 p.m. EST), with his head cradled in my mother's arms and his family praying by his side, my father left us to worship his beloved Christ in heaven, with the angels and that "great cloud of witnesses"—the many faithful Christians already with their Savior. It has thus been my sad honor to complete a few editorial odds and ends and to watch over the process of getting this book to press.

In the last weeks of his life, my dad (never known for his musical talent) made a reputation for himself as a singer. Comforted by the hymns sung by his family and his friends from Trinity Church, he was so eager to sing Christ's praises himself that he sang in the emergency ward, right through his oxygen mask. By the time he was settled into his hospital room, the nurses were whispering, "That's the man who was singing in the emergency ward!" My father's voice did not end with his death. This volume, with the others he wrote, will sing on: "I will declare your name to my brothers; in the congregation I will praise you" (Ps. 22:22).

Rebecca Clowney Jones
Escondido, California
January 2007

PREFACE

Each summer in southwest Philadelphia, where I was raised in a row house before the days of air-conditioning, I attended vacation Bible school at Westminster Presbyterian Church. There, when I was ten years old, I worked hard to memorize the Westminster Shorter Catechism, so that I could receive my Scofield Reference Bible—with a real leather cover! I used it for years, gleaning much from its notes. But as I read and studied that Bible, I came upon a confusing note about the Lord's Prayer. It told me not to pray the Lord's Prayer because it was not for the church age. If I used it, I would be praying on "legal ground." This prayer was given only for the millennial reign of Christ, when Christians would again be back under the law. Only then could we pray to have our sins forgiven on the basis of our righteousness in forgiving our debtors.

That advice didn't sit right with me. After all, I had just memorized all those Shorter Catechism questions about the law of God and the Lord's Prayer. The catechism assumed that I was still to take seriously God's commandments: Q. 42: "What is the sum of the Ten Commandments?" Answer: "The sum of the Ten Commandments is: To love the Lord our God with all our heart, with all our soul, with all our strength, and with all our mind and our neighbor as ourselves." The Catechism also recommended the Lord's Prayer. In relation to forgiving others, the Catechism had taught me: "We pray, That God, for Christ's sake, would freely pardon all our sins; which we are the rather encouraged to ask, because by his grace we are enabled from the heart to forgive others."[1] I was left puzzling over the question: What place *do* the Ten Commandments now have in the Christian life?

THE SCOFIELD BIBLE AND ITS INFLUENCE

Until the Scofield Reference Bible was published, most Bible study had been shaped by doctrinal formulations, supported by proof texts. The Scofield Bible, however, paid attention to Bible history and the epochs or periods in God's revelation. As a ten-year old, I did not understand the differences between Dr. Scofield and the men who prepared the Catechism that I had worked so hard to memorize. The Scofield Bible taught dispensationalism, emphasizing the differences between periods in biblical history. Actually, the idea of periods or eras was not foreign to the Westminster standards, since the Westminster Divines emphasized the periods of salvation history, even using the word "dispensation." The Westminster Confession distinguishes between the covenant of works, made with Adam in the Garden of Eden, and the covenant of grace "wherein he freely offered unto sinners life and salvation by Jesus Christ. . . ."

God's grace runs straight through the Old and New Testaments, as a constant, inexhaustible flow. Yet God administered his covenant of grace differently in the time of the law and in the time of the gospel. The Confession concludes the chapter on God's covenants by saying, "There are not, therefore, two covenants of grace differing in substance, but one and the same under various dispensations." The Confession recognized that God *administers* the way of salvation in particular periods, using the word "dispensation" in the sense of "administration."

On this issue, J. Nelson Darby, a Plymouth Brethren scholar in England, went further than the Westminster Assembly. He taught that dispensations differed in *substance*, and that different time periods therefore offered different *means* of salvation. In Darby's view, the Mosaic covenant was one of *works*—keeping the law under this dispensation would earn salvation. The covenant with Abraham, however, was a covenant of *promise*. This is the more radical view of different "ages" that I was discovering as I read my Scofield Bible. According to this approach, the Old Testament writers could not foresee the "church age." Their prophecy clock stopped when the church age began. When the Jews rejected Jesus, a parenthesis began in the history of prophecy. The covenant of law was suspended, and will return only when Jesus comes again in the millennium, at which point salvation will again be by works—in obedience to Christ, who will be reigning on the throne of David.

Such a reading of the Scriptures has been called the "dispensational" view. This view strongly emphasizes the differences between each era. Although it has often been dismissed (for it does have dangers, as we will see), it did serve a purpose for many Christians by giving them a valuable sense that the Bible presented a worldview. To read the Bible correctly, one has to understand its overarching structure. As I matured in my own faith, I came to see that not everyone understood the Bible's structure in the way the Scofield Bible presented it. Many argued forcibly that grace must always be the source of salvation. As time went on, many dispensational teachers began to change their views from those of Darby on that central point.

REFORMED-DISPENSATIONAL DIALOGUE

That subject now seems out of date. Many Christians today do not know what the word "dispensational" means, or what importance it still plays in our thinking about the world. It has had great influence, however, on the way Christians think about the law in particular, and also about other aspects of the Christian life. There was a time when dispensationalists and Reformed Christians had little time for each other. Recently, however, they have found more common ground.

Realizing that God's grace must always operate in salvation, many dispensationalists no longer teach that salvation was by works in the Old Testament. This realization has opened dialogue with Reformed seminaries, which had always vigorously opposed dispensationalism on this point. Another factor encouraging dialogue is the growing appreciation for Biblical Theology in Reformed seminaries. Reformed thinkers came to see that the Bible does not have the form of a dictionary. The Bible presents stories, stories that are all bound up in one, over-arching story. So, as dispensationalists affirm that God's grace is the fountain of salvation in both Testaments, and as Reformed thinkers teach about the history of salvation, both camps have come together to appreciate the unfolding riches of God's revelation in Scripture.

"Biblical Theology" is the term now used in the special sense of theology that is not only biblical, but is drawn from the history of revelation in the Bible. The *Westminster Confession of Faith* and the *Larger* and *Shorter Catechisms* followed the topical method, beginning with the question, "What is the chief end of man? Man's chief end is to glorify God, and to enjoy him forever." The teaching of the Bible is summarized topically: "The Scriptures principally teach what man is to believe concerning God, and what duty God requires of man."

Biblical Theology, in contrast, summarizes the teaching of the Bible by following the history of God's revelation in the periods or epochs of God's work in creation and redemption. Biblical Theology follows the *story* of the Bible rather than the *topics* found in the Bible. As a discipline of study, Biblical Theology was brought to this country from Europe, particularly Germany and the Netherlands. At Princeton Seminary, Geerhardus Vos (1862–1949) taught the discipline to students who later taught at Princeton Seminary and Westminster Seminary.

THE NEVER-ENDING STORY

From the book of Genesis on, the Bible follows the story of the Seed of the promise—the Son of the woman who must come at last to crush the head of the Serpent. To trace the history of redemption in the Bible story, we must recognize the periods or epochs of that story. Dispensationalism rightly recognized differences between these periods. However, it erred when it allowed the differences to break the continuity of the covenant story.

I have touched on the differences between my Scofield Bible and the Westminster Catechism, but my original question remains. What role *does* the law play in this history of redemption? If the law of Moses cannot offer salvation by works, how does it prepare for the coming of Christ? Why did God demand obedience to his law, if it could never serve to bring us to him?

Jesus showed that the law revealed by God in the Old Testament was itself a kind of prophecy, a part of the history of the covenant. That history, including the law, pointed to what was to come. In this sense, Jesus fulfilled the law not only by keeping it perfectly for us, but also by transforming our understanding of it. Christ not only obeyed the law, but also displayed its true meaning and depth.

Take the Great Commandment, for example: "Love the Lord your God with all your heart and with all your soul and with all your mind" (Matt. 22:37). Jesus transformed both that commandment and the second like it: "Love your neighbor as yourself" (Matt. 22:39). Jesus' interpretation of this law and his application of it in his own life is radical. He redefines everything from the term neighbor to the meaning of loving God. Jesus' love for God the Father was so great that he was willing to be accursed by the Father in order to carry out his Father's plan of salvation for those the Father had given him. Jesus' love for his neighbor was so great that he gave up his life for those "neighbors" (who hated him). Such a deep and radical notion of the law shows us the true demand of the commandment: to pick up a cross and follow him. As Jesus transforms this greatest of all commandments, he shows us a new level of interpretation for all of God's law. Without Jesus, we can have no true understanding of the law.

JESUS TRANSFIGURES THE LAW ON THE MOUNT OF TRANSFIGURATION

When Peter, James, and John were blinded by Jesus' glory on the Mount of Transfiguration, they also saw Moses and Elijah talking with Jesus. But neither Moses (the great lawgiver) nor Elijah (the most powerful of the prophets) added any word of explanation for Jesus' disciples. The Father's voice from the cloud said it all: "This is my Son, whom I love. Listen to him!" (Mark 9:7). Jesus did not come to supplement or to explain the law, nor only to live by it. He came to *fulfill* the law, in the deepest sense. To hear the Father's will, we must hear Jesus. He fulfills and transforms all the law and all the prophets. Indeed, he *is* God's new law!

1

THE COVENANT LORD
FULFILLS THE LAW

Jesus and the Ten Commandments

�֍

In late August and early September of 2003 the national media followed the story of the "Ten Commandments Judge." Judge Roy Moore, then the chief justice of Alabama, was dismissed from his office because he refused to remove a large stone monument bearing the words of the Ten Commandments from the Alabama state judicial center in Montgomery, Alabama. Judge Moore was ousted in response to a suit brought by the American Civil Liberties Union.

Jay Sekulow of the American Center for Law and Justice had responded to an earlier suit by the American Civil Liberties Union with an ingenious defense. A granite copy of the Ten Commandments had been placed in a park in Elkhardt, Indiana. When the ACLU brought suit, Sekulow did not plead that the Ten Commandments are not the creed of any particular church, but only a general statement of morality that has been part of Western political history from its beginning. Such a plea

is no longer acceptable in American courts, where the wall between church and state has put each body into its own hermet-
ically sealed chamber. Instead, Sekulow argued that the slab's
purpose was not religious, but secular and commercial. It had
been installed by Cecil B. DeMille to advertise the Hollywood
movie in which Charlton Heston as Moses came down Mount
Sinai, saw the idolatry of Israel, and threw down the stone slabs
of the Ten Commandments. How ironic that God's commandments, given to be a reflection of the divine character, should
be defended in our courts by eviscerating them not only of their
religious implications, but even of their moral ones!

Those who brought suit were right when they recognized
the religious nature of the Ten Commandments. Had the ACLU
been able to find a lawyer who knew his Bible, it could easily
have proved the commandments' inextricable link to the God
of Abraham, Isaac, and Jacob! (Mr. Sekulow knows that, too,
but his defense shows that he knows our courts as well—courts
that require public atheism as the meaning of the separation of
church and state.)

A TREATY DOCUMENT BETWEEN GOD AND HIS PEOPLE

The context and the text of the Ten Commandments are
unlike any other moral code or legal document. They are written to establish the separate and unique identity of the people
with whom God established a covenant agreement. The Ten
Commandments are a treaty document, written to define and
secure the oath of loyalty that Israel swore to God. Like many
treaties, this one concerned a nation, in this case the nation
that God had delivered from Egypt to lead to the Promised Land.

Our society observes treaties of various sorts. There are
business treaties, treaties between countries, and binding

legal agreements between individuals—such as the marriage treaty (though it has lost its binding nature in our nation's thinking). The Ten Commandments are part of a treaty that God made with his people. As scholar Meredith Kline has shown, the Ten Commandments in Exodus (repeated in Deuteronomy) have a literary form common to ancient Near Eastern treaty texts. In a preamble, the suzerain lord gives his name and claims the loyalty of his vassal. He cites the benefits he has bestowed, and states the treaty terms and stipulations. One demand is central. The vassal must be exclusively committed to the suzerain ruler. There may be no dealing with any other king, nor may the terms of the treaty be altered. The gods are summoned as witnesses to the treaty text. Faithfulness to the treaty will bring rewards, but treaty-breaking will bring the wrath of the great king.

This treaty pattern is followed in Exodus 20, and the treaty is renewed in Deuteronomy 5. The Lord, however, does not need to call on the gods of the nations to witness his treaty; the tablets of the law are in themselves his witness. The ark of the covenant is called the Ark of Witness (Ex. 25:16; 40:20 EPC). From the mountain, Sinai, God speaks the words of the law as his testimony, and he writes his treaty on the tablets of stone he provides (Deut. 4:10–14). The law is God's *Torah*, his covenant manual for life in the land.

In Deuteronomy, Moses tells Israel that when they enter the land, they are to set six of the tribes on Mount Gerizim to declare all the blessings that will follow obedience to the covenant law. The other six tribes are to recite from Mount Ebal the curses that will scatter them among the nations if they are disobedient (Deut. 28). Ultimately, however, in spite of Israel's unfaithfulness, God's purposes of mercy will not fail. God's final blessing will rest on his redeemed people (Deut. 4:30–31; 30:6).

As the history of Israel unfolded, the prophecies found in the law were realized. There were renewals of the covenant—at Shechem under Joshua (Josh. 24); at the coronation of David (2 Sam. 5); at the dedication of Solomon's temple (1 Kings 8); and at the Passover celebrated under Josiah (2 Kings 23). Had Israel remained faithful, such renewals would not have been necessary. But as their faithless rebellion ran its course, they constantly disobeyed, repented, reformed, and fell again into sin.

After Solomon, the kingdom was divided, and Jeroboam, to emphasize the independence of his kingdom, repeated the idolatry of the golden calf at Sinai. The Lord sent prophets, early and often. Elijah led the Lord's attack on the worship of Baal, calling down fire from heaven, but fleeing in discouragement from the wrath of Jezebel, the wife of King Ahab. Jehu's sword and Elisha's ministry continued the Lord's judgment on baalism. At last God used the Assyrians to conquer Samaria and sweep the Israelite idolaters into exile. While God's people were in exile, the prophet Ezekiel described the adultery of the two sisters: Oholah (Israel) and Oholibah (Judah). Using graphic images of adultery, he condemned the sin of Judah as even worse than the idolatries of Israel (Ezek. 23).

THE KING'S PROMISE

The history of Israel is, indeed, an indictment of man's inclination to evil. Yet God had promised that his covenant love would triumph. He would go far beyond the physical signs he gave his people to remind them of his person and character. He would circumcise their hearts and keep his covenant pledge (Deut. 4:20–40; 7:6–9; 8:2–6; 10:12–22). When Solomon dedicated the temple, he blessed God for keeping all his promises to Moses. The time of blessing had been followed by the time of judgment, as God's predicted wrath fell on Israel for its sin. But God did not abandon his people to judgment. In his mercy, he promised salvation in the "latter days" (Deut. 4:30 KJV). Ezekiel's vision saw the people of God in a great valley. The people were not gathered in joyful, worshiping assembly, however. They were all dead. In fact, their bodies had decomposed, and even their skeletons were not intact. All that remained of God's assembled people were their bones, scattered over the valley floor. "Son of man, can these bones live?" the Lord asked his prophet (Ezek. 37:3). Ezekiel was too wise to answer in the negative. He replied, "O Sovereign LORD, you alone know." On God's command, Ezekiel prophesied, an earthquake shook the valley, and the bones assembled. A well-known spiritual has it: "the head bone connected to the neck bone; the neck bone connected to the backbone—hear the Word of the Lord!"

Nothing short of resurrection life can deliver lost sinners from the wrath their sins deserve. Without it, they are no more able to live than could those heaps of dry and scattered bones. When Nicodemus did not understand the new birth, Jesus expressed surprise. How could this teacher be unaware of Ezekiel's prophecy that God would sprinkle defiled sinners with cleansing water and give them new hearts, and his Spirit (Ezek. 36:24–27)?

God's promise of salvation will include Sodom, Samaria, and the Philistines when God forgives all that his people have done (Ezek. 16). During the dark times of God's judgment, the prophets speak not only of restoration, but of renewal. God will preserve a remnant, and will restore and renew his people. No human king, not even David, could blow a trumpet to raise the dead. In Tolkien's fantasy *The Return of the King*, Aragorn, the rightful king, enters the underworld and summons the dead to follow him into battle. Tolkien's picture brings to mind the army that Christ leads from the death valley in his resurrection. Only the Lord himself, the true King, can bring the promised salvation. The situation is too desperate for anyone else to remedy; the promises are too great for any other to fulfill.

THE KING AS PROMISE-KEEPER

As the Lord's redemption unfolds in the writings of the prophets, we are dazzled by the glory of the promised fulfillment. The promises, as always, are too good to be true! "Come, buy wine and milk without money" (Isa. 55:1); "there will be one king over all of them and they will never again be two nations" (Ezek. 37:22); "I will rejoice in doing them good and will assuredly plant them in this land" (Jer. 32:41). Hundreds of such promises spill from the pages of the prophets.[1] But the key to their fulfillment is that God himself must come; his coming will bring victory and glory beyond description.

Isaiah gives us the divine names of the Servant of the Lord, and tells us of his saving work and triumph. His work will restore all that has been ruined and destroyed. He will gather and heal his own scattered sheep of Israel, and judge the shepherds that have so cruelly mistreated them (Ezek. 34:11–31). He will end injustice and oppression; as he moves into battle against evil, armed with his breastplate of justice and his helmet of salvation, he will deliver his people by his own saving righteousness (Isa. 59:15–21). Having conquered, he will spread his banquet table and gather not only the scattered of Israel, but also hosts of Gentiles to the feast on his holy hill. Egyptians will go to Assyria to worship the Lord, and Assyrians will go to Egypt. Gentile, enemy nations will be named as God's own people: "Blessed be Egypt my people,

Assyria my handiwork, and Israel my inheritance" (Isa. 19:25).
He will bring at last a new heaven and earth (Isa. 66:22).

The Lord who restores will also renew. The Servant of the
Lord dispenses from the treasure of God's Word truths both new
and old. In Christ the old things take on new life and new meaning. Yet, in him, all that is new is also old. When Jesus arrives to
fulfill Old Testament prophecy, he brings a New Covenant, the
kingdom of the King. He does not, however, wipe out the old.
Rather, his coming brings the dawn that the Old Testament
promised. Jesus said, "Do not think that I came to destroy the
law or the prophets. I did not come to destroy but to fulfill. For,
Amen, I say to you, till heaven and earth pass away, one jot or
one tittle will by no means pass from the law till all be fulfilled"
(Matt. 5:17–18 EPC).[2] We always put "Amen" at the end of a prayer
or doxology. Jesus puts "Amen" at the beginning of his statements, giving his words the solemnity of an oath. No need for
red letters! What Jesus taught was new, in contrast to rabbini-
cal teaching from the law: "You have heard that it was said to
those of old . . . but I say to you" (Matt. 5:21–22 NKJV).

JESUS: THE FULFILLMENT OF THE LAW

Yet Jesus insists on the continuation of the Old Testament covenant. Jesus says that the very letters of the law will
not pass away until all is fulfilled. As long as heaven and earth
exist, the law will endure. Jesus does not speak only of en-
durance, but also of fulfillment. We tend to think of the law
as rules to *obey*, but Jesus sees the law as something to *fulfill*.
Matthew's gospel often speaks of a particular Old Testament
passage being fulfilled. Jesus came to fulfill the Law and the
Prophets, for both the Prophets and the Law prophesied until

7

John (Matt. 11:13). John brought the last prophecies pointing to Jesus; with Jesus the fulfillment came.

Jesus fulfills the law by obeying it, but also by revealing its promise. When Jesus comes, the law takes on a different meaning and function. Its role of prophecy ends, for Jesus is the end (the *telos*, the goal) of the law. For this reason, once Jesus has come, God's people will never think of the law in quite the same way. We must not miss this *prophetic* function of the law. As we have seen, God's law is not given as an abstract moral code. Such a code would not be prophetic. God's law is given in the course of his saving work, and the whole of that work is leading us to Jesus Christ. The fulfillment of the law came when Jesus came and will continue until Jesus comes again at the end of this age.

Jesus fulfilled the law, then, not simply by obeying it, but by transforming it. Matthew's gospel shows us how Jesus transformed the law in his teaching. To understand this, let us think of how Jesus transforms the summary of the law.

Jesus makes astounding statements about the law. In interpreting our love for neighbors, he has the audacity to include our enemies in the definition of *neighbor* (Matt. 5:43–48)! What about his definition of our love of God? In Jesus we see how the law of love is transformed, for the perfect love of God is the love in which he gave his one and only Son to die for sinners. It is further defined as the love of the Son for the Father. In love for the Father, Jesus took the cup the Father gave him in Gethsemane, and drank it to the depths as he hung on the cross. It is in love for God that Jesus gave himself, but it is also in love for us. Only as we begin to taste and understand that love can we realize what it means to love without reserve. How profoundly Jesus deepens and transforms the love commandment at the cross!

In the pages that follow, we will consider how Jesus Christ transforms each of the Ten Commandments in his fulfillment of them.

STUDY QUESTIONS

Think It Through:

1. Jesus said that not one jot or tittle (the smallest stroke or the smallest letter) in the law would pass away until all was fulfilled. How did Jesus fulfill the law? How did it point to him?

2. What is the "first and greatest commandment"? How did Jesus fulfill it?

3. What is the "second like it"? How did Jesus fulfill it?

4. How did Jesus deepen the first commandment as he fulfilled it?

5. The climax of Old Testament prophecy is the promise that God himself must come. What made it necessary for the Lord to come?

Take It to Heart:

1. In what ways do you struggle with the place of God's law in your life as a Christian?

2. How has your understanding of the Ten Commandments changed as you have matured in your Christian life?

3. If you have been a Christian for a long time, do you feel as if you are better or worse at keeping God's commandments?

4. Do you feel at times as if the Lord is distant from you? At what times do you most feel his presence?

5. Is the Lord near you when you are not aware of his presence?

6. What experiences in your life have shown you that the Lord is truly with you?

7. What comfort do you derive in reflecting on Jesus' fulfillment of the Ten Commandments?

2

THE FIRST COMMANDMENT

One God and Savior

✦

And God spoke all these words: "I am the LORD your God,
who brought you out of Egypt, out of the land of slavery.
You shall have no other gods before me." (Ex. 20:1–3)

We have biblical background for the phrase "mountaintop experience." The Bible often speaks of mountains, and God marks his glorious presence by drawing his people's eyes upward to the mountains. Two mountaintop experiences frame God's revelation of himself to his people. The thunder and lightning of the Old Testament experience at Mount Sinai have been depicted in many a piece of art and in many a film. God's terrifying presence, the threat of death, the fearful quaking of the people—all these are physical signs of the importance of what happened on the mountain in the Sinai peninsula. God spoke, and declared his law to his people, revealing his person, his presence, and his commands.

Many years later on another mountain, in an incident recorded in the New Testament, God spoke again. The terrible, glorious, frightening, exhilarating cloud of the glory of God's presence once again overshadowed those on the mountain. Three disciples stood transfixed as they saw Moses, the scribe of the law, and Elijah, the representative of the prophets, speaking with Jesus. Moses, who had not been allowed to enter the Promised Land, found himself once again on the mountain with God. But this time, he was allowed to see the fulfillment of all that he had first witnessed on Mount Sinai. Instead of ten commandments, written on tablets of stone, and shattered at the foot of the mountain because of the people's sin, God uttered only one commandment—the true summary of the Law and the Prophets: "This is my Son, whom I love. Listen to him!" (Mark 9:7).

Jesus reveals the *I AM* God in the fullest possible way. The law is only a pale reflection in comparison. The Ten Commandments, God's first specific, verbal revelation of his nature to his people, help us to understand him and to understand his Son, who is the fulfillment of that law. So let us turn our attention to the first commandment.

I AM: THE GOD OF YOUR FATHERS

This first commandment determines all others that follow, for in it God defines himself, establishing his identity, and his right to speak commandments for us to obey. He does not begin with a tome of systematic theology, or with arguments from philosophy. He starts in history, and defines himself as the one who rescued his people from Egypt, fulfilling his promise to their fathers: "I am the God who brought you out of Egypt."

Many years before his revelation of the law to Moses on Mount Sinai, God had already set the scene. Remember that Moses, though he had been adopted by an Egyptian princess, identified himself with the people of God by striking down a taskmaster who had killed a Hebrew slave. As a result, Moses was forced to flee to the desert to escape a capital charge against him. There in the desert, the Lord appeared to Moses when he turned aside from tending sheep to see a bush that was burning without being consumed. From that fire the Angel of the Lord had warned the inquisitive Moses: "Do not come any closer . . . Take off your sandals, for the place where you are standing is holy ground" (Ex. 3:5). The Angel identified himself as the God of Moses' fathers—the God of Abraham, Isaac, and Jacob. He is Yahweh, the *I AM* God, who had heard the cries of the Hebrew slaves in Egypt and was going to act in their behalf. Moses could not deliver the people, though he had tried when he killed the Egyptian slave driver. It was God who had to act to deliver them.

JESUS: GOD THE REDEEMER

God's words to Moses at the burning bush seem too good to be true. God said, "I have come down to deliver my people" (Ex. 3:8). Four centuries before speaking to Moses, God had already told Abraham about the four hundred years of slavery that his children would endure, but also about the great deliverance that he would provide. From the bush, the Angel of the Lord instructs Moses to deliver God's merciful word to the people. When "they heard that the LORD was concerned about them and had seen their misery, they bowed down and worshiped" (Ex. 4:31). God cares. God loves. God delivers—and the people worship him for that salvation. The same Lord who came down at the burning bush is the Lord who later came down at Sinai to establish his covenant with his people. The mountain blazed with fire and smoke. Lightning shot from the cloud. Crashing thunder reverberated. The blast of heaven's trumpet heralded the presence of the Lord. The whole mountain became holy ground. The earth shook because the Creator had come down to his creation and to the human creatures he claimed as his own. The story of that rescue mission is the story that drives the entire Old and New Testaments. The redemption is not completed on Mount Sinai, for God's presence there is not the final expression of his saving work.

I AM: THE *I AM HERE* GOD

The *I AM* God identifies himself as the Redeemer, and his redemption is not done by proxy. It implies his personal presence. He is the *I AM HERE* God. Already God's power was made visible in the judgments he brought on Egypt, judgments that forced Pharaoh to release his grip on Israel. But God didn't leave it there, allowing his people to wander off, without a shepherd, into the desert. God brought Israel out of Egypt to gather them in his presence at Sinai. The fire of the Lord's presence had illumined the cloud that guided and protected Israel as they traveled.

God brought Israel to a trysting place with him in the wilderness. He said, "I carried you on eagles' wings and brought you to myself" (Ex. 19:4). He freed them from slavery in Egypt so that they could serve him as their Lord and God. The covenant God made with them at Sinai shows why he brought them there. He claimed Israel as his own, so that he would be their God, and they would be his people. This is the kind of God he identifies himself to be in this first commandment—a personal God who delivers, accompanies, and owns his people (Hos. 2:14).

JESUS: GOD INCARNATE

How could anything surpass the thunderous wonder of God's coming down at Sinai? There is nothing, it would seem.

In the Prophets, however, God promises even more. More marvelous than the height of heaven or the stretch of eternity is another coming of the Lord. The same prophets who denounced the sins of Israel proclaimed that one day the Lord himself would come in person to deliver his people. These promises were fulfilled when the Lord came down at Bethlehem, and the virgin Mary wrapped him in swaddling clothes and laid him in the straw of a cattle feed trough.

Hints of this amazing birth are given in the Old Testament. When Sarah, the wife of Abraham, heard the Lord's promise that she would have a son in her old age, she laughed to herself, just as Abraham had fallen over laughing at the same promise. The Angel of the Lord asked, "Why did Sarah laugh . . . ? Is anything too hard for the LORD?" (Gen. 18:13–14). When Mary would also ask, "How will this be, . . . since I am a virgin?" (Luke 1:34), the angel Gabriel was to answer with the same words: "For nothing will be impossible with God" (Luke 1:37). The Lord came as the Savior of his people.

JESUS: GOD WITH US

The Angel of God's Presence came at various times in the Old Testament, but his appearances only foreshadow the ultimate presence of God as manifested in the birth of the Savior in the line of David. In the law spoken from Sinai the Lord identified himself as "the LORD your God." When Jesus comes to do his Father's work (John 5:19–23), he is more than a servant, working on God's behalf. He speaks not only *for* God, but *as* God, for he speaks the very words of his Father: "I am telling you what I have seen in the Father's presence" (John 8:38).[1] John's gospel reveals Jesus to be the Logos, the Word of God who is not only God's eternal Fellow, but God the Son himself

(John 1:1–18). Jesus pushes his enemies on this very issue, emphasizing his lordship. He is not another servant in the line of human prophets. He quotes Psalm 110:1: "The Lord said to my Lord: 'Sit at my right hand until I make your enemies a footstool for your feet' " (Luke 20:42–43). Then Jesus said, "David calls him 'Lord.' How then can he be his son?" (Luke 20:44). The *Son* of David, Jesus, is the promised *Lord* of David who came as David had prophesied in the psalm. Jesus said directly, "Before Abraham was born, I am!" (John 8:58).

God can say in this first commandment that he is *our* God because of his eternal plan to come as *our* Savior and take on *our* flesh.

JESUS: GOD THE BRIDEGROOM

The presence of the *I AM HERE* God is not a mere formality. We are not in his presence the way a guest sits at a political banquet, far from the President's table, unable to have even a brief word with him. God intends an intimate relationship with his people. In fact, the Old Testament already shows us the intimacy of the relationship that God intends to have. He is our God by being our Bridegroom: "As a bridegroom rejoices over his bride, so will your God rejoice over you" (Isa. 62:5b). God, the faithful husband, will come to seek and redeem his people, who are guilty of constant adultery against his loving claim on their lives. John the Baptist described himself as a friend of the Bridegroom and pointed the penitent to the Bridegroom who came from heaven (John 3:29). Jesus explained that his disciples did not fast because the Bridegroom was still with them: "The time will come when the bridegroom will be taken from them; then they will fast" (Matt. 9:15b). In the parable of the ten virgins, Jesus is the Bridegroom who will return to those

who wait for his coming. The God we worship in the first commandment is a perfectly loving husband to us. He comes in person to woo us, care for us, and rejoice over us.

JESUS: GOD THE KING

The "souzerain king" of the Old Testament treaty comes
to his people in person. The King comes in the person of Jesus,
who is the King and Judge in the kingdom of God. He is the Son
of Man[2] in Daniel's vision (Dan. 7) who comes on the clouds of
heaven to receive an everlasting kingdom. Jesus is plainly
speaking of himself when he says, "When the Son of Man comes
in his glory, and all the angels with him, he will sit on his throne
in heavenly glory. All the nations will be gathered before him,
and he will separate the people one from another as a shepherd
separates the sheep from the goats" (Matt. 25:31–32).

JESUS: GOD'S IMAGE

On a mountain one day, Peter, James, and John saw the
radiance of Jesus' glory. Brilliant light streamed from his face
and his robe. They must have begun to understand how Jesus
fulfilled the Law and the Prophets as Moses and Elijah stood
there beside Jesus—Moses representing the Law, and Elijah the
Prophets. These representatives of the Old Testament Covenant
spoke with Jesus about his exodus, which was his saving deliverance through the cross. The same cloud of God's glory and
his presence that had enveloped Sinai enveloped them on this
mountain. In the terror of that darkness, the disciples heard
the voice of God—the same voice that had sounded from Sinai.
At Sinai God had spoken ten commandments. On the mountain of Jesus' glory, the voice of God the Father spoke only one
commandment: "This is my Son, whom I have chosen; listen to

him" (Luke 9:35). It was not an eleventh commandment, a kind of appendix, or even an amendment to the law. When Jesus came, it was to fulfill the law, which he did by perfectly fulfilling the very first of the Ten Commandments: "You shall have no other gods before me."

JESUS: ONE WITH THE FATHER

The process of self-revelation of which Sinai was a part ("I am the God who . . .") reaches its culmination in the exact image of God in the incarnate Christ. No longer do we ask, with Philip, "Lord, show us the Father" (John 14:8). We have the answer of Jesus:

> Don't you know me, Philip, even after I have been among you such a long time? Anyone who has seen me has seen the Father. How can you say, "Show us the Father"? Don't you believe that I am in the Father, and that the Father is in me? (John 14:9–10a)

The first commandment says, "You shall have no other gods before me." Jesus says, "I am the way and the truth and the life. No one comes to the Father except through me" (John 14:6). Only the Father knows the Son, and only the Son knows the Father and those to whom the Son chooses to reveal him (see Matt. 11:27). The apostle John writes, "And we are in him who is true—even in his Son Jesus Christ. He is the true God and eternal life. Dear children, keep yourselves from idols" (1 John 5:20b–21). Jesus claims the worship that God himself accepted in the Old Testament. That Jesus shares the identity of God is evident in what Jesus said to Philip—he is in the Father and the Father in him.

In addition to claiming the worship due only to God, Jesus proves his identity by doing the saving work that only God could do. He is the Good Shepherd who gives his life for the sheep. Ezekiel pointed to the love of God, the Shepherd, who sees his people scattered like sheep on the mountainsides, prey to wild beasts. The Lord says, "I myself will search for my sheep and look after them" (Ezek. 34:11). Jesus both seeks and saves the lost, and leads them in and out, calling his sheep by name.

Jesus claims those the Father has given him in his High Priestly Prayer (John 17). The petition he makes astounds us: "I pray also for those who will believe in me through their message, that all of them may be one, Father, just as you are in me and I am in you" (John 17:20b–21a). The unity of believers is unity with the eternal Son of God, who is himself one with the Father.

JESUS: GOD THE SUFFERING SERVANT

We have seen that only God could come to do his saving work. To do his redeeming work, Christ must be true God and true man. Jesus was therefore born of the Spirit in the womb of Mary. But incarnation is insufficient to redeem. When the Ten Commandments were given as the seal of the covenant agreement between God and his people at Sinai, the blood of sacrifice was sprinkled on the altar, on the law, and on the people. We have seen that the altar sacrifice was at the heart of the covenant. Israel's worship centered on the sacrifice as the substitute for the sinner. Isaiah picks up the theme of sacrifice in his prophecy, emphasizing especially the work of the suffering Servant, who takes the punishment for our sins. By his wounds we are healed, and he must pay the cost of redemption. Abraham was able to spare his son Isaac from the altar, since God provided a substitute, in the form of a ram caught in the bushes. Ultimately, however, there could be no substitute animal when the Father dealt with our sin. He could not spare his own Son, but had to deliver him up for us all. Jesus, God the Son in his human nature, can alone pay the infinite price of our redemption. Jesus is the Lamb of God: the Lamb given by the Father (Gen. 22:8; John 1:29; 1 Peter 1:19).

JESUS: GOD THE CONQUERING SAVIOR

Isaiah sees not only the suffering Servant, but also God as the conquering Savior. Since the leaders of Israel cannot protect them, God says he will put on his helmet of salvation and breastplate of justice to deliver them (Isa. 59:15–21). John's gospel emphasizes the victory of the cross. Jesus says, "Now is the time for judgment of this world; now the prince of this world will be driven out. But I, when I am lifted up from the earth, will draw all men to myself" (John 12:31–32). The cross that lifted Jesus a few feet from the ground began the victory that raised him to the right hand of the Father. Jesus claims the saving victory of divine lordship. He fulfills the claim the Lord makes in the law: "I am the LORD your God, who brought you out of Egypt, out of the land of slavery." The physical deliverance of Israel from Egypt was a type of the victory of Christ. "And having disarmed the powers and authorities, he made a public spectacle of them, triumphing over them by the cross" (Col. 2:15).

JESUS: NO OTHER GOD, NO OTHER NAME

The first commandment demands devotion to the one God as it is expressed in devotion to the Son, who alone shows us the Father. "No other gods" means no other name than the name of Jesus. In no way does this detract from the Father, to whom Jesus taught us to pray, but we take the very name "Abba" from the lips of Jesus.

The presence of the Lord at Sinai revealed his love for his people. Love is the bond that made them his, and he theirs. Moses gave the great summary of the law: "Love the LORD your God with all your heart and with all your soul and with all your strength" (Deut. 6:5). Jesus repeated that command. He gave it the full meaning that only he could bring. We know love because the Father, in his love, gave his Son, not only in Bethlehem, but on Calvary. The flame of our love is kindled at his altar.

And so we see that this first commandment, "You shall have no other gods before me," is fulfilled in our Lord Jesus, whom God identifies as his beloved Son. In "hearing him," we honor the first commandment, for in worshiping him we worship the one and only true God, who delivers us from Egypt and from the captivity of our sin. Conversely, anyone who fails to worship Christ cannot be worshiping the one true God.

But a question remains. Is there a danger in placing *too* much honor on Christ? Do we perhaps dishonor the God of Sinai if Christ becomes the focus of our worship?

STUDY QUESTIONS

Think It Through:

1. Moses asked the name of the Angel who appeared to him in the burning bush. What name did the Angel give him? (Ex. 3:13–14)

2. Why did Abraham fall on his face, laughing at the promise of God? Why did the Lord spare him? (Gen. 17:17ff.)

3. What question about Psalm 110:1 did Jesus put to his enemies? (Luke 20:41–44)

4. In Isaiah 62:5, the prophet promises that God would have the joy of a bridegroom in his relationship with his people.

John the Baptist uses *Bridegroom* as a title for Jesus. What does this use of terms show about John's claim for Jesus?

5. How did Jesus answer Philip's request to "show us the Father"? (John 14:8–9) What are some other passages in John's gospel that show the deity of Jesus?

Take It to Heart:

1. What Scripture passages have rekindled love for God in your heart?

2. Which hymns have moved you to a deeper appreciation of the love of God?

3. What idols have you found in your own heart that have quenched your love for the Lord?

4. Have you recently been touched by God's love? Was it in hearing the preaching of the gospel? In suffering? In comfort from other Christians? In public worship? At the communion table? In morning devotions? If you are using these questions in a group context, perhaps you would be willing to share one of these experiences with the others in your study group.

3

THE SECOND COMMANDMENT

We Worship the Exact Image of the Invisible God

"You shall not make for yourself an idol in the form of anything in heaven above or on the earth beneath or in the waters below. You shall not bow down to them or worship them; for I, the LORD your God, am a jealous God, punishing the children for the sin of the fathers to the third and fourth generation of those who hate me, but showing love to a thousand generations of those who love me and keep my commandments." (Ex. 20:4–6)

Harry Emerson Fosdick, a famous modernist at Riverside Church in New York City, once preached a sermon on "The Peril of Worshiping Jesus." According to Fosdick, worshiping Jesus is idolatry, since Jesus was a man. Was Fosdick right? Do we break the second commandment by worshiping the image of

God, instead of God himself, when we worship Christ? After all, the second commandment forbids us to make images and worship them.

THE IMAGE OF GOD IN MAN

The second commandment cannot mean that there never has been or will be an image of God, for the Lord God made *man* in his image (Gen. 1:26ff.; 5:1-3; 9:6). Theologians have debated over what it means that man is in the "image" of God. Some have argued that since man is distinguished from other mammals by his reasoning ability, reason is what makes man the image of God. The neo-Kantian philosopher Ernst Cassirer, in his *Essay on Man*, had another idea. He decided that language is man's distinctive quality. Animals only signal to one another, but they do not form symbols. (More recent research on chimpanzees has found that even they have some grasp of symbols.) Recent discussions of God's image have sometimes focused on the male–female distinctions, grappling with how God's image could be complete in human beings who are so different. Some go so far as to reason that there is no God distinguishable from the creation and that human beings are therefore not in his image at all, but are rather an expression of God, as are all other created things.

THE SOUL AND THE BODY

For the sake of our argument in this chapter, we will assume that there is a "God who is there," as theologian Francis Schaeffer put it,[1] and that he created man to reflect his nature. Explanations of man's qualities as being the "image of God" are insufficient if they focus uniquely on the physical or intellectual aspects of our human nature. The New Testament makes clear that it is the soul of man, not his reasoning ability or his physical features, that makes him a person in the image of God. Scripture distinguishes between the soul and the body. Jesus said to the thief on the cross, "I tell you the truth, today you will be with me in paradise" (Luke 23:43). Surely this has to mean that Jesus and the thief would be together apart from their bodies, since Jesus' body would remain three days in the grave. But is the soul the only part of man that is in God's image? Jesus rose from the dead in his body. He left the tomb and greeted Mary Magdalene on Easter morning. To demonstrate that his risen body was real, he ate a piece of fish, smiling, perhaps, as he chewed it. All of this seems to emphasize the importance of the body as a part of God's image. Can it be possible that the body is a part of the divine image in man?

This body–soul union and distinction is puzzling. Our souls or spirits may rejoice with the Lord apart from the body. Paul said, "I desire to depart and be with Christ, which is better by far; but it is more necessary for you that I remain in the body" (Phil. 1:23–24). Yet Paul also says, "We do not wish to be unclothed but to be clothed with our heavenly dwelling, so that what is mortal may be swallowed up by life" (2 Cor. 5:4). The Lord does provide a form in the intermediate state for his redeemed in heaven before the resurrection. We were not created as disembodied spirits. After God had said, "Let us make man in our image, in our likeness" (Gen. 1:26), he formed Adam "from the dust of the ground and breathed into his nostrils the breath of life" (Gen. 2:7). We are made body and soul, and our redemption cannot be complete until the resurrection of the dead, when we receive our resurrection bodies (2 Cor. 5:4). Man in his body–soul created state is made in God's image. God chose to reflect himself in human beings, both male and female.

ONLY GOD CREATES IMAGES OF HIMSELF

The second commandment affirms that only God can make an image of himself. It does not forbid us from making images of the things God created. In fact, God instructs his people to make "images." For example, God himself designed the tabernacle, but he ordered that images of angels (presumably represented in human form) be woven into the curtains of the tabernacle (Ex. 26:1).

In our day, biotechnology is exploring the manipulation of the human genome. Although the stated goal of such research is to correct hereditary illness or deformity, it may eventually try to create different forms of human or semi-human life. Cloning has risen to the fore in our scientific discussions as society grapples with the morality of creating "copies" of human beings. Research on human cloning advances, in spite of many laws forbidding it. Several research institutes and medical schools are experimenting with "chimeras," hybrid forms created by introducing human stem cells to developing animal fetuses.[2] Though one might argue that such a representation is still only a manipulation of the image God made, one day we will be toying with a completely artificial human attempt at "creating" humans. This attempt to create a new image of God would violate God's command, for only God has the right to create his image. Whether God will allow us to disobey this command is somewhat speculative. We are not sure what the results will be if men "create" other men. In Revelation 13:11 and following, we read of an image of the beast that is given breath and is able to speak. Our descendants may well have to deal with complex ethical questions that will demand a thorough understanding of this second commandment.

THE IMAGE OF GOD IN CHRIST

A true understanding of the second commandment must come as we look at Jesus, who transformed it. Jesus shows us the richness and depth of this commandment when he answers the hypocrites who ask him, "Is it right to pay taxes to Caesar or not?" In response, Jesus asks to be shown a denarius, a coin used in paying Roman taxes. "Whose portrait is this?" he asks his opponents. "And whose inscription?" They were forced to reply, "Caesar's." As he always did in his responses to their provocation, Jesus avoids the trap and forces them to deal with the true meaning of God's law: "Give to Caesar what is Caesar's, and to God what is God's" is his stunning answer (Matt. 22:17–21).

In recognizing the authority of Rome, Jesus makes an enormous transition from Old Testament theocracy to a new notion of kingdom. But he goes much further in this simple statement about a Roman coin. It becomes obvious that he is teaching us to give back to God what bears his image, just as people had to give back to Caesar the coins that bore his image. If Caesar gets a coin, what does God get? We give God back his image by giving him ourselves.

Jesus understands this better than any other human being, for he is the primary bearer of that image. He bore God's image completely: "In Christ all the fullness of the Deity lives in bodily form" (Col. 2:9). Jesus was not only a true human being, a real man, and therefore in the image of God. He was also incarnate by the power of the Spirit, working in the womb of Mary. We have seen that as true man, he was and is also true God. The incarnate Christ is not a human attempt to create an image of the living God. Christ is God's gracious gift of an anointed image, which we are not only permitted but commanded to worship.

The incarnate presence of Christ fulfills the second command-ment, which, like the others, contains an element of *promise*.

THE PROMISE OF THE SECOND COMMANDMENT

When the law was proclaimed at Sinai, the Israelites saw no image of God. They only heard a Voice (Deut. 4:12). The picture of God was not complete. We see the same element of incom-pleteness in the ark of the covenant in the Holy of Holies, which was kept in the tabernacle. It had a lid of gold on which there were figures of two cherubs. Even when the glory of God rested above the cherubim, the lid on the ark, known as the "mercy seat" (KJV), was vacant. That void contained a promise. The One must come for whom that seat was reserved. The throne is reserved for Jesus Christ. No man or idol can sit in that holy seat. The jealous love of God will not tolerate idols, for God will send his own image, his incarnate Son (Ex. 20:5; 34:13), to occupy the empty seat.

JESUS: GOD IN A BODY

Only God can make his own image. God commanded men not to make an image of him, but the implied promise in the sec-ond commandment is that God *would* make an image of himself. He did not want his people trying to make an image of him be-cause his purpose was to show himself to his people in the person of Christ. The fulfillment of the second commandment is the birth of Jesus Christ. His incarnation, the author of Hebrews tells us, is anticipated in Psalm 40:6–8 (in the Greek Old Testament): "Sac-rifice and offering you did not desire, but a body you prepared for me." How are we to view that body? Can we break the second com-mandment by worshiping images of the body of Christ?

Everything that Jesus did revealed the Father. Though we have no portrait of Jesus, we do know what Julius Caesar and other historical figures looked like. Artists of that time painted portraits and carved sculptures. Yet it is no accident that the Bible does not give us a vivid physical description of Jesus, for we are not encouraged to enter into a new form of idolatry by worshiping physical pictures of the image of God in Jesus Christ, any more than the Old Testament worshipers were encouraged to worship pictures of God.

When I was a student at Yale Divinity School years ago, I saw in another student's room a devotional center with the popular Sallman portrait of Jesus between two candles. There was no Bible. This attempt to create a "mood" for worship is similar to the attempt that many make in hanging crucifixes above the altar, or in the alcoves of churches. But we do not need pictures or physical symbols of the image of God as it is expressed in Christ.

Thousands have professed faith in Christ after seeing the "Jesus" film distributed by Campus Crusade for Christ. Yet the appeal to come to Christ is made by an actor calling to the viewer, "Come to me!" The camera zooms in on the face, then the eyes, of the actor. It would seem that the actor is himself the Jesus to whom we are called. Another film shows the reality of Jesus' sufferings by showing the actor actually bearing the beatings and lashings that Jesus endured, and hanging on a cross for as long as he could stand it.[3] The most recent and most popular by far of such media representations of Christ is the movie *The Passion of the Christ*, produced by Mel Gibson. Here again, an actor graphically portrays the reality of Christ's physical suffering.

PORTRAITS OF JESUS?

These attempts at portraying Jesus' life in a realistic manner may have gone overboard in depicting Jesus and risk inviting a kind of idolatry. But they rightly emphasize the physicality of Christ. We are now living in a society in which "Christ" has come to mean anything and nothing. Take, for example, the comments of a professor of religious studies at Brown University in a PBS documentary entitled *From Jesus to Christ*:

> It's less important to me to know exactly . . . what happened to [Jesus] than to understand the impact that shifting images [of] Jesus have had on Christianity . . . Even if the ultimate historical Jesus is unknown or unknowable, nevertheless, the Jesus of myth or the Jesus of image, the "believed in" Jesus, or the Christ of faith, is a historical figure, because we can trace that figure as influence . . .[4]

Retired Bishop John Shelby Spong puts the same idea in the following words:

> Christ has been and still is many things to many people. All of them are Christ and none of them is Christ. Freeze any image and idolatry is the sure result. Allow no concrete images to emerge and the Christ will disappear from our consciousness.[5]

We do not commit idolatry when we "freeze" the image of God as it was in the physical person of Jesus Christ. If we follow the principles expressed by these thinkers, Christ will indeed disappear from our consciousness, for God has told us in his Word what Christ we are to worship. It is the Christ who was born of a woman, who died, and who was raised again. We must not bow to the pressure exerted on us as Christians to remove physical reality from the revelation of Jesus. Such pressures are not unique to our times. An early error with regard to the incarnation was the Docetic heresy, the teaching that the physical nature of Christ was only an appearance, not solid flesh. The Gnostics also denied the physicality of Christ, claiming that the true Christ sat on a tree laughing, as Jesus (a substitute) was put to death on the cross. You have probably met friends and neighbors whose definition of Christ rejects the physical birth, death, and resurrection of Jesus. In our desire not to profane Christ by worshiping an image of him, we must also be cautious that we don't "spiritualize" him into thin air. If we show no pictures of Jesus' everyday life to our children, how will they know his reality?

Let me offer a principle that may help us determine what is a good use of image when it comes to portraying Jesus. I suggest that *portraits* of Jesus are the problem. Many representations show the reality of Jesus without offering a portrait, which in its very nature invites us to worship. To look at Jesus' face is to worship him.

Rembrandt painted Peter's denial of Christ. The painting shows Peter facing a woman who has recognized him as a Galilean, and therefore as one of Christ's disciples. The scene is the courtyard of the house of the high priest. In the foreground on the left the gleaming armor of a Roman soldier catches light from a fire and from the torch held by Peter's accuser. The painting is masterful, as we see, for example, in the almost translucent flesh of the servant's hand as she holds the torch. But off in the distance, at a higher level, stands Jesus on trial before the Jewish authorities. He is barely discernible, but he is looking at Peter. Rembrandt's composition achieves what seems impossible. That small figure, away from the light and almost in the corner of the picture, is the focus of attention. Your eye, caught by the flashing armor and the torch and face of the woman, is swept along to the figure of Jesus. As I stood looking at this painting in the Rijksmuseum in Amsterdam, I was moved to tears.

The painting tells the story most eloquently, without falling into the trap of presenting a portrait, which might draw away from, rather than encourage, our worship of Jesus. Countless pictures of Jesus in children's books achieve this same balance. Because the artists use the same formula for all faces, they are in no sense attempting an accurate portrait of Jesus' face. More modern drawings solve the problem by creating semi-cartoonlike images, which are in no danger of being considered exact representations. This theory may have some support in the importance God seems to put on face-to-face encounters. When God allowed Moses to "see" him, he passed by, allowing Moses to see only his back. While I don't wish to make too much of this principle, it is wise in dealing with pictorial presentations of the gospel to portray the physicality of Jesus realistically without creating an icon that itself becomes the focus of worship.

Christian worship is heavenly, and although Jesus had a real body, with a real face and distinctive physical characteristics, representations of his physical body are not to be the focus of our worship. We pray to the real Jesus where he now is. We reach children's hearts not by offering them crayons to draw Jesus, but by showing them how to talk to him. He is real, and is not a picture.

THE CHURCH AS THE IMAGE OF CHRIST

Yet Jesus fulfills the second commandment in a more breathtaking way. By the power of his Spirit he unites us to himself, so that we are remade in his image. Our union with Jesus is union also with his Father. Nothing stands between the Father, the Son, and the Spirit. The unity of the persons of the Trinity surpasses our understanding. Neither can we comprehend Jesus' prayer for our unity with the triune God: "that all of them may be one, Father, just as you are in me and I am in you. May they also be in us" (John 17:21). We know, however, that our personal union with Christ is the ultimate purpose of God's design in making us in his likeness. Jesus Christ is "the image of the invisible God, the firstborn over all creation" (Col. 1:15); "for in Christ all the fullness of the Deity lives in bodily form" (Col. 2:9). The coming of Jesus transposes the second commandment into specific adoration for the one who is the image of the Father. That same miracle of grace also draws us to praise God for the imaging of Christ in the lives of those brothers and sisters in whom the Spirit works.

IDOLATRY, PHYSICAL AND SPIRITUAL

To recognize the image of God in Christ and the image of Christ in his beloved church is not idolatry. Of course, we *are* to worship Christ, and we *are not* to worship the church, which is made up of created beings. True idolatry, so hated by God, is the worship of anything or anyone other than God (Father, Son, and Holy Spirit). Idolatry is the great sin charged against Israel in the Old Testament. God's jealousy was aroused when his people worshiped other gods, idols that pretended to represent him. When Aaron gave the people of Israel a golden calf to worship at the foot of Mount Sinai, he appointed a feast to the Lord, confusing God's people by allowing them to believe that they could still worship God while bowing down to a calf. The Lord would not accept such worship. When Moses came down from the mountain, he confronted these idolaters. Only his own tribe, the Levites, rallied to Moses when he cried, "Who is on the LORD's side?" (Ex. 32:26 KJV).

Isaiah, the prophet, mocked idolaters. From the same log they carved the image of an idol and chopped firewood to cook

33

their supper. Idolaters to this day claim that an idol is only a symbol and not the object of their devotion, but idolaters soon go beyond the symbolic. In any case, even if the worship is supposedly intended for him, the Lord God will not accept it if it is focused on an idol. The Father has offered us a true image to worship, and his jealousy is aroused if we choose anything but the incarnate Lord Jesus as the focus of our worship. Jesus is the true and only object of worship.

A generation ago, we saw little evidence of physical idols in most Western countries. As goddess- and earth-worship have come back into vogue, however, more and more signs of physical idols appear around us. A trip to your local mall will probably show you statues of Buddha, Quexicoatl, several Hindu and Egyptian gods, and plenty of cats, snakes, and fetishes. Four of my great-grandchildren live in what was formerly East Berlin, where their parents work as church-planters under a mission board. In the park where my granddaughter takes the children to play stands a huge statue of Baal. Such idols will become more evident as our society turns from worshiping the Creator and the image he provided in Christ to worshiping the creation. The recent trend toward witchcraft often involves "familiars" that become the voice of spirit guides to those who use them. Some deep-relaxation techniques, even in elementary schools, encourage children to choose spirit guides to aid and counsel them. The Old Testament injunction against such idols is easier for Westerners to understand now than it was thirty years ago because in cultures highly influenced by Christianity, we could see no blatant evidence of physical idolatry.

Avoiding such statues, however, does not guarantee that we are keeping this second commandment against creating images of God and worshiping them. To establish any idol in our hearts is to forsake him. An idol is defined not only as a physical representation of God, but as anything that functions as a focus for our worship, even if it has no physical representation. Whatever has the place of Jesus Christ in our heart is an idol. In fact, we are probably more tempted to worship nonphysical idols than totem poles or statues of Buddha. The love of money and the desire for power serve as functional idols and are less easily identifiable as such.

Even mature Christians feel the tug toward idolatry. Whatever we add to worship that God has not commanded also draws us toward this sin. Our worship must be biblical, for though we cannot now see Jesus, we can hear him, for he has given us his Word. (Remember the one great command given on the Mount of Transfiguration: "This is my Son, whom I love. Listen to him!" (Mark 9:7).) His Spirit illumines the Word to our understanding, and the preaching and teaching of his Word are means that the Spirit uses to open our hearts for worship. True worship is active adoration of the Father through his Son. His Spirit not only prays for us, but draws us to prayer. And our worship is both physical and spiritual.

We are told to worship God in all that we do. Paul speaks of offering our bodies as a sacrifice, which is our spiritual act of worship (Rom. 12:1). As we worship Christ, we worship God made flesh. How appropriate that he inspires us through his Spirit to have both a heart of worship and a body that offers itself in acts of worship, as we dedicate ourselves to obeying the second commandment.

ACCEPTABLE WORSHIP IN CHRIST

As we conclude this chapter on worshiping God, may I speak a word of encouragement to you, my dear brothers and sisters in Christ? If you have been a Christian for any length of time at all, you will have realized that the farther you walk along the road of Christian maturity, the more you realize how desperate your own sin is. As you read these lines about true worship, you may feel discouraged. "How can I ever truly worship God and annihilate the idolatry of my own heart?" you will ask. Let me encourage you to realize that as you are *in Christ*, you are also *worshiping God in him*. As you are *in the Spirit*, your worship is *acceptable in God's sight*. We come before the throne not for judgment, but for blessing. In Christ, God can accept your worship as perfectly pure and without idolatry. So do not hesitate to offer your Father in heaven the worship that is in your heart. In Christ, his perfect image, it is purified, is made perfect, and is a pleasing aroma to God.

STUDY QUESTIONS

Think It Through:

1. Does the image of God in man include his body?

2. Were there any likenesses to created beings in the tabernacle made in the wilderness?

3. Why was there no image between the cherubim on the golden lid of the ark of the covenant?

4. Why do we have no portrait or statue of Jesus, made during his life on earth?

5. Should an artist today paint a portrait of Jesus for a worship center?

6. What defines an idol?

Take It to Heart:

1. Meditate together on John 5:18–21. (Meditation can involve reflection and discussion!)

2. How do you grow in knowing Jesus Christ? Describe an experience you have had of knowing truth *about* Jesus without knowing Jesus.

3. Find a gospel passage in Matthew, Mark, or Luke that recounts something Jesus did. How does the passage help you to know him? Worship the Lord together, praising him in light of the passage.

4

THE THIRD COMMANDMENT

Reverencing the Name of God

"You shall not take the name of the LORD your God in vain, for the LORD will not hold him guiltless who takes His name in vain." (Ex. 20:7 NKJV)

You've probably heard a Christian mother or father explaining to a child that a movie is not suitable because there is "too much swearing" in it. Often, our understanding of the third commandment is limited to such a case. Although we don't like foul words, Christians are particularly bothered, and rightly so, by the careless and needless use of God's name, which is often spat out, whether in a film or in real life, by godless people in a fit of anger or spite. As do all the commandments, however, the third has much broader implications.

HONOR, MORE THAN A NAME

The third commandment is a general commandment with broad application. In their translation of the third commandment, the NIV translators use the phrase "misuse the name of the LORD your God" rather than "take the name of the LORD your God in vain." The commandment gives a general statement, which is made specific in other places in the Torah. One specific case of misuse is dishonoring God's name by using it in a false oath.[1] Another is sacrificing a child to the god Molech,[2] and a third is using God's name for magic or sorcery.[3] If you are using this book as a group study guide, you can refer to the questions at the end of the chapter for insight on some other actions that are specifically tied in the Old Testament to the dishonor of God's name.

The name of God is much more than a combination of letters or sounds. After all, God's name is different in Russian than it is in English. If we say the word *bog*, we mean a swampy area, whereas in Russian it means "God." When the Bible speaks of God's name, it is not indicating that a particular set of letters carries some mystical power. The name of God is the Bible's way of speaking of God's presence in his revelation. Using God's name is a serious act not because certain sounds are holy, but because God himself is present in his name, and all his works reveal that name. In this sense it is impossible to dissociate God's name from his person, identity, and character. When the Angel of the Lord personally revealed the presence of God at the burning bush, he told Moses that his name was "Yahweh" (Ex. 3:14–15). The Angel that led Israel in the wilderness bore God's name and was to be feared as divine (Ex. 23:20–23). That Angel of the covenant who appeared was the Son of God, the second person of the Trinity. God is not distant and unknowable, but personal. He allows us to speak to him by name and reveals his character to us.

Judaism so feared misusing the name of God that the Jews permitted only the high priest to speak the name, and only on the Day of Atonement. In the Old Testament, however, the name of God is used often. To "call on the name of the LORD" became a synonym for worship (Gen. 4:26b). When priests would bless the people, they would do so by putting God's name on them (Num. 6:22–27). The psalms use God's name and propose its use in song and praise on the lips of God's people. The prophets would authenticate their message by claiming its revelation from God and placing his name on their pronouncements as a kind of validating signature.

REVERENCE FOR THE NAME

As he does with the other commandments, Jesus heightens the third commandment by deepening the reverence to be shown toward God's name. He warned against using the name of God in oaths. Jesus told his disciples not to swear at all, but simply to say "yes" or "no" (Matt. 5:33–37; James 5:12). The implication seems to be that if the name of God is dwelling in a believer by the Spirit, then the believer's word should be as good as God's and need no extra swearing. The testimony of a believer should be backed up in his godliness by the testimony of God himself! In short, a believer's words and character should be as trustworthy as those of the living God. We do not have the place for an extended discussion of oaths here. There may still be some place for lawful oaths.[4] But Jesus' point is that God's name is a living reality with implications in every area of the life of his people.

THE NAME "FATHER"

Jesus transforms the third commandment in another way, by revealing the name of God as "Father." To be sure, the term *father* had been applied to God in tribal religions. The progenitor of the tribe was a deified "father." The Greek poet Homer spoke of the "Father of men and gods." In the Old Testament, God is seen as Father of his people, for Israel is the firstborn

41

son of God (Ex. 4:22ff.). Moses' song asks, "Is he not your Father, your Creator, who made you and formed you?" (Deut. 32:6b). Malachi brings the Word of God to his people: "If I am a father, where is the honor due me? If I am a master, where is the respect due me?" (Mal. 1:6).

Only occasionally does the Old Testament use the term *our Father* (e.g., Isa. 63:16; Mal. 2:10), though it gives us glimpses of the fatherly love of God. The loving bond of father and son shines out in such narratives as that of Isaac, the beloved son of Abraham, who must be sacrificed. King David is inconsolable at the death of his rebellious son, Absalom. His cry is heart-wrenching, and familiar to any of us who have children: "O my son Absalom! My son, my son Absalom! If only I had died instead of you—O Absalom, my son, my son!" (2 Sam. 18:33b). The Lord himself cries out in passionate love for his children. He exclaims his love for Israel his son: "How can I give you up, Ephraim? How can I hand you over, Israel? . . . My heart is changed within me; all my compassion is aroused" (Hos. 11:8).

JESUS AND HIS FATHER

More powerful than the foreshadowing of the Old Testament is the freshness and fullness of Jesus' relation to his Father, which overwhelms us. He prays to the Father as the Son. Jesus knows the Father, has been sent by the Father, speaks his Father's words, and does his Father's deeds. Jesus prays, "I praise you, Father, Lord of heaven and earth, because you have hidden these things from the wise and learned, and revealed them to little children." He goes on to claim: "No one knows the Son except the Father, and no one knows the Father except the Son and those to whom the Son chooses to reveal him" (Matt. 11:25–27).

The Son of God opens the door of heaven to make the third commandment new to us. The familiar and intimate term he uses for God his father (*Abba*, the equivalent of *Papa*) is a term he places on our lips, giving us full rights as sons! He teaches us to pray, "Our Father in heaven" (Matt. 6:9). We may call out "*our* Father" to *his* Father, who resides in the heights of glory. In the very first petition that Jesus teaches us to pray, we are to say, "Hallowed be your name." Holiness is the heart of the Father's glory and the essence of his name. "Glory" means the Father's exaltation beyond all creation and all understanding. He is "God, the blessed and only Ruler, the King of kings and Lord of lords, who alone is immortal and who lives in unapproachable light, whom no one has seen or can see" (1 Tim. 6:15–16). There is no one like him. He is holy because he is the one and only God, set apart in a place of his own. Yet he has decided to share that glory with us, by setting his name on us. So we, too, are "holy," set apart in our own place to bring honor to his name.

MAKING GOD'S NAME HOLY

We see that in order to obey the third commandment, it is not sufficient to keep ourselves from swearing, or even to remain silent. We are to name the name of God and confess its holiness. How can we possibly "make holy" the name of our Father in heaven? Is he not forever holy beyond all description or praise? Our Father must make holy his own name. He does that not only by revealing what he does but by being who he is. Yet Jesus takes us by the hand and brings us before the throne of the holy God. We ask our Father to show his glory, his holiness, his righteousness both in judgment and in salvation. That name, that glory, that praise is seen as God's kingdom comes, and as his will is done in earth as in heaven. What is so overwhelmingly marvelous is the fact that Christ gives God's name to Christians. We bear that name, for in baptism, our name-giving ceremony, we receive the name of the Father, the Son, and the Holy Spirit. We receive the name of the triune God as our name, our family name, our Father's name.

As we carry the name of the Father, we also carry the name of the Son. Jesus taught us to pray to the Father in his, the Son's, name. We come to the Father through the Son because Jesus promises to pray for us in glory. His name has been lifted above every other name, and Jesus shares the glory of the Father. Jesus' name is no less than the name of the Father. When Jesus gives us his name, we are automatically receiving with that name the name of the Father and the Spirit. Just as the name "Father" sums up all the names of God in the Old Testament, so the name "Jesus" also fulfills the promise of the Old Testament names of God, for God says that he will not share his glory with another; yet he shares it fully with Christ Jesus.

THE NAME OF JESUS

The name "Jesus" fulfills all the promises attributed to the name of God in the Old Testament. Jesus speaks the *saving* power of the Son of God. Jesus rules over all the angelic hosts, which are placed under his feet and serve us for his sake (Heb. 1). Jesus is, therefore, Yahweh Sabaoth, the Lord of Hosts. He is El Shaddai, for he is the Almighty God who uses his omnipotence to accomplish his purpose of salvation. He appeared to Moses, as we have seen, as the Angel of the covenant and identified himself as Yahweh, the *I AM* God, who uses his divine power in salvation. The Son of God incarnate said, "I tell you the truth, before Abraham was born, I am" (John 8:58). To Abraham, the Lord revealed himself as "Yahweh Jireh," the Lord who sees, or sees to it, providing the sacrifice instead of Isaac. "On the mountain of the LORD it will be provided" (Gen. 22:14). Jesus is the one who made the provision; he is the sacrifice.

So, too, with other names for God. Many are connected with events in the history of redemption: Jesus is the God of Bethel; he is El-Elohe-Israel, God the God of Israel, taking the name of his people into his own name. The names of God in the Old Testament point us forward to fulfillment in Christ.

JESUS CLAIMS THE NAME

Some may have trouble understanding how shocking Jesus' earthly ministry must have been to the Jews. He was not content to call God's people back to God. Rather, he had the gall to call them to *himself!* As he preached the coming kingdom, he preached his own coming: "today this scripture is fulfilled in your hearing" (Luke 4:21). Before Pilate, on trial, Jesus was asked under oath, "Tell us if you are the Christ, the Son of God." Jesus answered, "Yes, it is as you say . . . But I say to all of you: In the future you will see the Son of Man sitting at the right hand of the Mighty One and coming on the clouds of heaven" (Matt. 26:64). The high priest tore his clothes and said, "He has spoken blasphemy!" (Matt. 26:65). Blasphemy, blasphemy! Indeed, Jesus' life and words are full of blasphemy—unless he truly is the God of glory, come to live among men.

Jesus knew that the name of God was his. He triumphantly bore that name throughout his earthly ministry, and even after ascending to heaven, he continues to bear it from his throne in glory. His name still bears the power of the Creator, the God of the universe. Jesus continues to show the power of his name. In the name of Jesus, his disciples healed the lame beggar at the Beautiful Gate of the temple. Peter explained: "It is Jesus' name and the faith that comes through him that has given this complete healing to him, as you can all see" (Acts 3:16b). The priests commanded the disciples not to teach in the name of Jesus. Peter replied that "there is no other name under heaven given to men by which we must be saved" (Acts 4:12). Philip baptized in the name of Jesus in Samaria, and the apostles confirmed the spread of the gospel to the Samaritans by praying that they might receive the Holy Spirit. The theme of the name of Jesus pervades the book of Acts, casting its enemies into a state of fear. Paul claims the power of the name of Christ to cast out demons.

CREATION GIVES THE NAME GLORY

The name of the Lord is revealed in all his works. Unbelievers look at creation and have a desire to worship, but they do not acknowledge the name of the Creator, to give him praise. Instead, they praise the creation itself, which does not have a name. Worshiping creation leaves us empty, for we do not know whom to thank for the great gift of a world that sustains us with its bounty and stuns us with its beauty. Creation speaks to us the name of the Father and the Son. Though even unbelievers have a sense of God's presence in creation and are counted inexcusable because of it, believers know God's presence in creation in a more intimate way because they know the Creator as he is revealed in Christ. "The heavens declare the glory of God; the skies proclaim the work of his hands. Day after day they pour forth speech; night after night they display knowledge" (Ps. 19:1–2).

> God, all nature sings thy glory,
> and thy works proclaim thy might;
> Ordered vastness in the heavens,
> ordered course of day and night;
> Beauty in the changing seasons,
> beauty in the storming sea;

> All the changing moods of nature
> > praise the changeless Trinity.[5]

That hymn also speaks of the disruption of sin, and of our personal praise to a God who offers salvation:

> Yet thy grace and saving mercy
> > in thy Word of truth revealed
> Claim the praise of all who know thee,
> > in the blood of Jesus sealed.[6]

Our praise and thanks go not to impersonal nature itself, but to a personal God with a name, who has revealed his power and goodness in creation, but who has also revealed his personal love to us in his Word and in his Son. This God who has given us his name and taken us into his family is the God whom Christians worship and whose name brings them delight.

CHRISTIANS CLAIM THE NAME

Though nature sings the name of the Father and his Son, it cannot claim God's name in the way we can. In and through Jesus, we who belong to him hallow and reverence the name of God, for he is our Lord and Savior. When we possess the name of Jesus as Christians, our understanding is transformed! Now we fulfill the promise of the Old Testament to "declare his glory among the nations, his marvelous deeds among all peoples" (1 Chron. 16:24). "At the name of Jesus every knee [shall] bow . . . and every tongue confess that Jesus Christ is Lord" (Isa. 45:23; Phil. 2:10). From the moment Peter began preaching at Pentecost until the Lord Jesus returns in glory, believers have been calling and continue to call on sinners to repent and be baptized in the name of Jesus Christ.

47

His name is written on our foreheads. In our praises, our prayers, our sharing of the gospel, we lift up the name of Jesus, the mark and power of our lives.

The protection of his name is crucial to our own well-being because our names are bound up in his; he has incorporated our names into his. In such verses as Exodus 3:16, God actually names himself as "the God of Abraham, Isaac and Jacob." In so doing, he binds these patriarchs to himself and thus to eternal life. The same is true for each of us on whom his name is placed. He is "the God of Barbara," "the God of Jimmy," "the God of Olaf," "the God of . . ."—fill in your own name, if you belong to him. Hallowing the name of our God and Father also protects our own identity, though we do not reverence it for that reason alone.

Practically speaking, there are many ways in which we can honor the great name of God. As with all commandments, we not only put off practices that dishonor God's name, but also put on attitudes of the heart and deeds of obedience that bring honor to that name. Keeping our hearts free from idols, claiming our children for the name of God, not seeking to know mysteries that are not revealed to us, believing in the continued power of the name of Christ to cast down the strongholds of evil, making sure that our "yes" has the solidity of God's truth behind it, never giving honor to anyone but God for the blessings he has given or for the beauty of creation—in these and in many other ways we obey the third commandment to honor the name of our God and Father.

STUDY QUESTIONS

Think It Through:

1. What are some of the names of God used in the Old Testament, and what do they mean?

2. Read the following passages and consider why God's name would be dishonored in the activities mentioned: Lev. 18:21; 19:12; 20:3; 22:2; Jer. 7:30; Ezek. 20:39; 36:22–23; Mal. 1:6ff.

3. God tells Israel to beware of the Angel leading them in the desert, "since my Name is in him" (Ex. 23:21). How can the Angel bear God's name? (Remember the burning bush in Exodus 3:2, 4.)

4. How did the priests of Israel put God's name on his people? (Num. 6:23–27)

5. In what sense is baptism a name-giving sacrament?

6. What does it mean to pray, "Hallowed be your name"? (Matt. 6:9)

7. What name for God was given by Jesus?

8. How did the apostles use the name of Jesus? (Acts 3:16; 4:12)

Take It to Heart:

1. Have you learned to rejoice in the name of Jesus? Take time together to praise the name of the Father, the Son, and the Spirit. Prepare for prayer by talking together about what these names mean for us.

2. We often pray in the name of Jesus as a formula. Pray silently or together, pleading the very name of Jesus in praise, thanksgiving, intercession.

3. Ask the Spirit to search your heart. Have you ever been ashamed of the name of Jesus?

5

THE FOURTH COMMANDMENT

Resting in the Lord

✦

*"Remember the Sabbath day by keeping it holy. Six days you
shall labor and do all your work, but the seventh day is a
Sabbath to the LORD your God. On it you shall not do any
work, neither you, nor your son or daughter, nor your
manservant or maidservant, nor your animals, nor the alien
within your gates. For in six days the LORD made the heavens
and the earth, the sea, and all that is in them, but he rested
on the seventh day. Therefore the LORD blessed the Sabbath
day and made it holy."* (Ex. 20:8–11)

In my desire to be a good father, I tried to help my children
understand that Sunday was a day of rest. I'm sure my attempts
were far from ideal, but one principle I tried to emphasize was
that we were not to engage in regular activities of play and work,
but to dedicate ourselves in specific ways to reflecting on Christ
and giving him that day in honor and service. My son certainly
understood the theory, but he was also extremely creative. One

Sunday, I surprised him playing dominoes. He quickly pointed to one side of the domino game. "Those are the Israelites," he stammered, "and these are the Philistines!"

LEGALISTS?

Jesus received criticism, too, on his use of the Sabbath, but he did not need to stammer out any excuses. It is perhaps the Sabbath commandment that shows most clearly how Jesus transforms the law. When Jesus' disciples followed him one Sabbath afternoon, they plucked heads of grain in the fields they were crossing. Rubbing the ears between their hands, they extracted the grain and snacked on it, to ease their hunger. The paparazzi do not track celebrities any more persistently than the zealous Pharisees tracked Jesus. The Jewish media were close enough on the heels of the disciples to notice this seemingly minor infraction of Sabbath commands not to work on God's day of rest. "Look!" they cried. "Your disciples are doing what is unlawful on the Sabbath" (Matt. 12:2).

How would we have answered their shocked accusation? "Such pettiness! How hairsplitting can you get? With their mind-set, these legalists never knew when to stop. To be sure, if one of the disciples had brought along a sickle, a charge of working on the Sabbath could be made. But how narrow-minded to view informal plucking as harvesting and hand-rubbing as threshing!"

With such an answer we must have sympathy. The Pharisees were legalists. Such attitudes can be found in our own time in a variety of religious settings. A friend of mine was in a Jewish synagogue in which a rabbi was expounding on the Sabbath. When asked if it was legal to load a dishwasher on the eve of the Sabbath, he responded that such an activity would not be considered work if the dishwasher were not loaded systematically by sorting the dishes. Throwing the dishes in pell-mell would be just fine!

The Pharisees were quibbling in the same way as the dishwasher rabbi and my creative son. They were not leveling a serious charge of Sabbath-breaking because they had very little understanding of the true meaning of the Sabbath. Jesus constantly pointed out their misunderstanding of Old Testament principles, and reprimands them again in this incident when he says a bit later, "If you had known what these words mean, 'I desire mercy, not sacrifice,' you would not have condemned the innocent" (Matt. 12:7).

What is it about the Sabbath that the Pharisees failed to understand? What does the Old Testament Sabbath imply? Why does God recommend that his people keep the Sabbath day holy?

OLD TESTAMENT SABBATH LAW

We do not know whether the Sabbath law was known in some form by God's people before he revealed it to them through Moses at Sinai. Whatever Sabbath-rest principle they may have had from their understanding of the creation, it seems unlikely that the Egyptian taskmasters would have respected it. The Sabbath law that God gave to his people on Mount Sinai was one of the Ten Commandments on the tablets that Moses brought down from the mountain. It was found in what we often call the first tablet of the law. In the Sabbath commandment, God is revealing a principle about himself and about his people. After Mount Sinai, the Sabbath became a part of the Old Testament calendar, set on the seventh day because it is the last of the days of the week and reflects the seventh day of creation, on which God himself rested.

So what is the significance of the Old Testament Sabbath?

PHYSICAL REFRESHMENT

The Sabbath was given for a variety of reasons. The most simple and basic, of course, is God's provision for bodily rest and refreshment. The people were not to work "24/7," a principle workaholics finally realize after their first heart attack. Some cultures have tried work cycles of four, ten, or fifteen days, for example, in an attempt to discover the most efficient rhythm. Apparently, such efficiency tests revert to a rhythm of six workdays followed by a day of rest. What a relief the hard-driven Israelite slaves must have felt when they realized that their God was not like their tyrannical slave masters in Egypt who would work them to death. He cared about their physical well-being and even provided a double measure of manna the day before the Sabbath, so that they would not need to work for their food that day. The broad law of the Sabbath forbade any work on the part of family members, servants, visiting strangers, or even oxen and cattle.

FELLOWSHIP WITH GOD

But God's rest is not just a parenthesis in the workweek for the good of the body. It carries a much deeper significance. God did not rest to recover from exhaustion, nor is his rest defined simply as an absence of work. His rest carries with it the sense of a positive, active appreciation and satisfaction in his finished creative work. In his rest, God is reveling in the goodness of his creation, and especially in the goodness of fellowship with those he created in his own image. God's rest is not an abstract principle that does not touch the lives of his chosen people. God gives Moses a blessing that he is to teach to Aaron and his sons: "The LORD bless you and keep you; the LORD make his face shine upon you and be gracious to you; the LORD turn his face toward you and give you peace" (Num. 6:24–26). This blessing shows that the peace and rest experienced by the people is the peace that comes because God is with them, among them, loving and caring for them. The blessing is God's presence, God's rest. The Sabbath marks the fact that God delights in the presence of his people. Of course, God's rest in creation is not the end of the story, just as the Israelites did not find true rest in their desert wanderings. The rest to which the Sabbath points is not only rest from the tyranny of Egypt but the rest they will know in having a true home, a land of their own, where they can live in peace and in the presence of God. God brought them *out of* Egypt *to* the Promised Land, their land of rest.

A SIGN OF REDEMPTION

God's creation rest and the Sabbath that marks it point to another rest—the rest of redemption. The Sabbath is the ordinance that expresses God's covenant with his people. It is a sign not only of creation, but of redemption. The Israelites keep the Sabbath as a memorial of their redemption from slavery in Egypt and of their being brought to rest in the land God promised them. The Sabbath looks forward to a complete and final rest in perfect communion with God. By marking out that day, God's children are reminded that they belong to God as physical creatures and depend on him for their very breath. They are also reminded that their purpose is not the labor itself so much as it is their communion with the God who made them.

A PEOPLE SET APART IN PLACE AND TIME

The Sabbath serves yet another purpose for Israel. It marks God's claim on the Israelites as his own people. They are a Sabbath-keeping nation. Their regular observance of their weekly holy day marked them out as belonging to God, in distinction from the pagan nations that surrounded them. This claim on them will one day be extended as God lays claim to many other people and nations. In this sense, the Sabbath is a sign not only for Israel, but also for the other nations whom God will incorporate in his rest. Isaiah tells of a day when God will say, "Blessed be Egypt my people, Assyria my handiwork, and Israel my inheritance" (Isa. 19:25). The beginning of the accomplishment of this promise is God's faithfulness in rescuing his people and in showing his grace and his power to bring them into God's Sabbath rest.

In the land God gave them, there was to be a holy *place*, the temple, where God would set his name, but there was also a holy *time*. We are perhaps more familiar with the idea that God set apart a particular *place* where his people would come to worship him when they came to the Promised Land. The temple pictured God's dwelling among his people as the holy place of his presence. God dwells in Zion. We are less familiar with the idea of a holy *time*. The pattern of seven was applied to the holy *times* of God's law. The seventh *day* is joined with the seventh (sabbatical) *year*, since the land was to lie fallow on the seventh year. After seven sevens of years came the year of Jubilee, the fiftieth year, which was the climax of the sabbatical system. As we examine Christ's fulfillment of the commandment to keep the Sabbath holy, we will see that he accomplished all the times of the Sabbath, the Sabbath year, and the final Jubilee, freeing all those enslaved by sin.

We see how rich the Sabbath principle is. It provided the people physical rest, which was a reminder of their created nature. It provided them with a reminder that God's presence offers them true rest. It reminded them of their redemption from slavery, and it held out a hope for them of a permanent rest to come, in the Promised Land. As the writer of Hebrews points out, however, "there remains . . . a Sabbath rest for the people of God" (Heb. 4:9). As history moves on, it becomes obvious that the physical land of Israel is not the final rest.

THE SIGN OF A GREATER REST

There is a deep spiritual meaning to the Sabbath. True rest can be found only in the presence of God. In the Old Testament, God leads his people from captivity through the desert to the land of rest. In that land, the people meet with him in his temple and find peace and protection in his presence. Even this rest remains a symbol of the final rest that comes with Jesus Christ. The Sabbath, then, not only looks back to God's rest after he had completed his work of creation (Gen. 2:2–3), but also looks forward to the final peace given through Jesus Christ.

JESUS ANSWERS THE PHARISEES: DAVID BROKE THE SABBATH, TOO

Now that we have seen some of the Old Testament principles concerning the Sabbath, we have a better foundation for understanding Jesus' answer to the Pharisees. When they accuse the disciples of breaking the Sabbath by picking a few grains of wheat from a field, Jesus does not simply say, "You're nitpicking!" As is so often the case, his answer surprises us. He does not dispute the charge of Sabbath-breaking, but compares his disciples' behavior to that of King David and his men when they were hungry. Fleeing from the wrath of King Saul, David and the men with him ate consecrated bread from the tabernacle—bread that only the priests could lawfully eat. Jesus also shows that the priests themselves worked on the Sabbath. Their service to the temple required them to "break" the Sabbath.

Why does Jesus find his disciples innocent? The answer shows how Jesus transformed the Sabbath command. He argues that the service of King David justified his eating the holy bread and giving it to his followers. The service of the temple justified the work of the priests in the temple. The analogy is completed when Jesus says, "I tell you that one greater than the temple is here" (Matt. 12:6). What had come? The kingdom of God, and the Lord of the kingdom, had come. If David's actions are justified because of the great service to which David was called, if the priests are justified because of the great service to which they are called, then Jesus' disciples are justified because they are called to an even greater, more holy vocation. Jesus claims to be greater than Jonah, greater than Solomon (Matt. 12:41–42), greater than the temple. In fact, Jesus is so great that he claims to "own" the Sabbath: "For the Son of Man is Lord of the Sabbath" (Matt. 12:8). In this incident, when he is accused of healing on the Sabbath, Jesus authoritatively defines what may and what may not be done on the Sabbath. Jesus defines Sabbath service, saying that it is lawful to do good. In serving Jesus, his disciples are automatically keeping the Sabbath, since there can be no greater service of the Sabbath than that given to Christ himself, who is the Lord of the Sabbath.

JESUS, THE LORD OF THE SABBATH

God's rest from the work of creation issued in his work of redemption, by which that creation would be renewed in Christ. As we saw, God gave the Sabbath to his people from Sinai to mark his lordship over them, to distinguish them from the surrounding nations, and to show them the plan of God for their redemption. The promise of rest in the land of Canaan was only a picture of the rest that Jesus, the Lord of the Sabbath, brings to the people of God. Jesus is the Lord of that rest. The Sabbath that was made for man was made for Jesus. We see how Jesus, when he had completed his work of suffering, could say, "It is finished" (John 12:30).[1] When Jesus said that, he was affirming that the end of his agony for us ushered in the beginning of his eternal rest as the risen Lord of all things. The memory of God's rest gives us an understanding of the blessing we receive as we are united to Christ in his heavenly triumph. When Jesus said that he is the Lord of the Sabbath, he was affirming that he is the Creator and the Redeemer.

If Jesus is the Lord of the Sabbath, if he is the Redeemer and Creator, then he also has to be the Lord of men, since the Sabbath was made for man and not man for the Sabbath. Jesus is the Son of Man, to whom is given the eternal kingdom. The Sabbath was made for Jesus because it foreshadows the rest that he brings. In the Sabbath of redemption, the Father is not resting but working, and Jesus, too, is hard at work, doing the work of his Father. So Jesus includes his servants in his work and hallows their sustenance in that work, seeing the Sabbath as the entire period of accomplishment of salvation. This understanding rings true of David and his followers, who were wearing themselves out in the service of God, to establish the king on his throne and to bring about the anointed kingdom of God. It rings true of his disciples, who find nourishment in the fields as they serve Christ, and it rings true for us today as we serve Christ and his kingdom.

Only united to Christ, the Lord of the Sabbath, can we fulfill all our Sabbath duties, finding rest in God's presence and entering into an eternal rest that satisfies all the hope of the original Sabbath day of rest. Not only will we find rest for our bodies, as they are transformed in resurrection, but we will find in Christ both our place of rest and our time of rest; we will find our freedom in a final jubilee year; and most of all, we will find eternal communion in the presence of our Creator and Redeemer. Such notions of the Sabbath were far from the unbelieving eyes of the Pharisees, but after Jesus' resurrection, his disciples began to understand the transformed Sabbath principles and to apply Christ's teachings in the church.

PAUL AND THE SABBATH

Paul had to deal with the question of Sabbath observance in churches with Jewish and Gentile believers. He instructed them not to judge one another on the matter of Sabbath observance. The Old Testament observances of feast days, New Moon celebrations, and the Sabbath day were all shadows of things to come in Christ. "The reality, however, is found in Christ" (Col. 2:17). Paul counsels those who understand this reality to show love and understanding to those who are weaker in the faith, and have not yet realized the change that Christ has brought (Rom. 13:8). "One man," writes Paul, "considers one day more sacred than another; another man considers every day alike. Each one should be fully convinced in his own mind. He who regards one day as special, does so to the Lord" (Rom. 14:5–6a).[2]

Yet we must not assume that the man "who considers every day alike" will show no interest in attending the gathering of the saints on the first day of the week. That man has reached a level of maturity at which he realizes that the service of Christ must be carried on just as intensively on Wednesday and Friday as on Sunday. He is the man who wishes that he could be with God's people every day of the week! The early church did meet together regularly on the first day of the week, and Paul elsewhere admonishes believers not to neglect these worship assemblies. The apostolic church met for worship on the Lord's

Day, the day of Jesus' resurrection (Acts 20:7; 1 Cor. 16:2), and we learn from the book of Revelation that John was in the Spirit on the Lord's Day (Rev. 1:10). In this sense the Sabbath rest is still celebrated: on the Lord's Day we find rest and refreshment in Christ and the richness of the eternal rest in which the Son of God is one with his people in the heavenly rest of his glory.

THE WORK OF THE KINGDOM IS REST

Christ brings spiritual rest. He calls to the weary and burdened to come to him for rest. Yet even in that invitation, Jesus showed the heavenly nature of his rest. The Lord's Day doesn't yet offer us the satisfaction and joy we will know in our final rest. Jesus promised rest to those who took his yoke. How can a yoke bring rest to the burdened? Christ's yoke is an image of his lordship. We labor under his authority and in his power. Because we are laboring for him and by his strength, we have his peace even though we have not reached our final rest. Jesus blessed his disciples with the peace that he alone can give. Jesus gives peace with God, and peace in living for him, not for ourselves. We may cast all our cares upon him, for he cares for us. This peace might seem illusory, however, were it not for the promise of final rest.

The author of Hebrews describes the future rest that awaits the people of God: the perfect rest of God that has no ending. That hope of heaven awaits us. It is the place where we will enter into the rest of God the Creator: a rest in which perfect love will cast out all our fears; a resting place prepared ahead of us by our older brother, who will wipe away every tear; and a resting place where there will be no more sin or suffering or pain or separation or loneliness.

In Christ, we taste already the rest and peace found in his presence. To go and be with Christ is far better, but through the Spirit we already know the gift of Christ's rest. God, who rested from his work of creation, still works in providence and redemption. Jesus, the Son of God, has entered his rest, but he now carries forward his saving work until the final heavenly rest is ushered in.

OUR RESTING SAVIOR IS AT WORK

Our first-day worship is part of our calling to do *more*, not less. Jesus' understanding of the law always expands and deepens our knowledge of what it means to honor and obey the Father. Paul understands this when he speaks, for example, of stealing. Paul shows the thief that not stealing is only the beginning of obedience. The next step is to find work so that he is actively producing something instead of taking what belongs to another. Yet even this is not full obedience. Not until the thief has left stealing behind, produced something by the work of his own hands, and given away what he owns, out of generosity and love, has he fully obeyed God's command not to steal! Jesus sets up these expectations for the Sabbath. Not only are we to leave aside our own preoccupations and entertainment on the first day of the week, not only are we to set apart time to worship God, but we are to serve the Lord with a full heart. We are to serve not only on the first day, but on every day that is given to us. It is perhaps in this sense that some count all days the same. Surely in Christ, every day is to be filled with worship and service of our King.

GOD'S REST FOR GOD'S PEOPLE TODAY

Though we do not fully understand what this commandment truly requires of us, we remind ourselves of God's call on our lives and of the dedication we owe him in worship and in service by not "forsak[ing] the gathering of ourselves together" (Heb. 10:25 NKJV). Jesus' disciples spent the very first "first day of the week" together, rejoicing in the resurrection of the Lord. On that first resurrection Sunday the disciples seemed hesitant to announce Christ's triumph to the outside world, so stunned and amazed were they. Later, however, they used the first day of the week to announce the good news of the gospel and to exercise acts of mercy and compassion, as Jesus had taught them to do by his own observance of the Sabbath. In our Christian worship, we come together as a gathered body of Christ to honor him, to remind ourselves and the world that we belong to him, and to announce the resurrection of the Lord of the Sabbath, who offers true rest to those who receive him. As we call one day "the Lord's," we must be careful to show the love of Christ in New Covenant service to others, as well as coming together for worship, rest, and refreshment.

The Sabbath cannot sanction idleness. The Lord's covenant does not call us to spend the first day of the week uniquely on Sunday-afternoon naps. Though physical rest is surely a part of the first-day observance, the Lord's Day is also a day of activity, to be celebrated by fulfilling the commission that the Lord has given us. The promise of rest is transformed by the fact that the seventh-day observance becomes a first-day observance. The celebration on the seventh day has been transformed by Jesus' resurrection. Christ's victory over the powers of darkness in his resurrection glory accounts for the shift in the New Testament from the seventh day of the week to the first day of the week.

To follow Jesus on the first day of the week is not only to keep the first day as the Old Covenant people of God were required to keep the seventh day. It is to consider the first day as united to Jesus Christ, our Savior, and to look for opportunities to show devotion to him in activity that we know pleases him in the work of the kingdom. Christians have, through the centuries, used the first day of the week in caring for the sick and the poor, the oppressed and afflicted, and those whom we may reach with the message and the healing comfort of the gospel. In particular, those who are elders of Christ's church or deacons ministering in Christ's name have the responsibility of enlisting the service of the church to care for those in need.

The shadow of the Old Covenant has become the reality in the fulfillment of Christ's compassion and the calling of the Great Commission. Jesus transforms the Sabbath to make the whole world see the fruit of the gospel in the company of believers. The world must see in the life of the church the compassion of Jesus Christ in social ministry and evangelism. We sometimes forget the impact that Christian service has made in the midst of the agonies of this world. As the world watches us fulfill God's commandment to keep the Sabbath day holy, they will see the resurrection power of Christ and get a taste of the rest into which God is calling his own.

STUDY QUESTIONS

Think It Through:

1. Jesus' disciples were picking and eating grains of wheat as they walked after Jesus through a grainfield. Would you consider that activity breaking the Sabbath?

2. On what grounds does Jesus defend his disciples? (Matt. 12:1–13)

3. What service justified David's men when they ate the bread taken from the table in the Holy Place? What service justified the priests who worked in the temple?

4. How does Jesus transform the Sabbath? What is his authority? Who is the Lord of the Sabbath? What is the day known in the church as the "Lord's Day"? (Rev. 1:10)

5. Why do we observe the day of the resurrection of Jesus Christ?

6. How does Paul counsel the church on Sabbath observance? (Rom. 14:5; Col. 2:16–17)

7. What does Hebrews 4:1–11 teach us about entering God's Sabbath rest?

Take It to Heart:

1. Reflect on what the Lord's Day means in your life. How could you make the day the Lord's? Talk about this together. What changes could you make that would make this day more to his glory? Does the Lord's Day offer opportunities in the Lord's service that children or young people could join? What place does physical rest have in the day?

2. How could you make every day like the Lord's Day? Should you?

3. Talk and pray together about the public worship of your church. If your delight is in private worship, have you learned to rejoice in public worship? Does the Lord's Day end for you at the benediction in the morning service?

4. Reflect on living with other Christians: service together in hospitals, prisons, and rest homes, and making friends with neighbors. Prize the time you spend with the Lord as a time that can be shared with other Christians.

6

THE FIFTH COMMANDMENT

The Family of God

"Honor your father and your mother, so that you may live long in the land the LORD your God is giving you." (Ex. 20:12)

Christians in America often use the phrase "family values" to describe biblical values, and such a term does keep the sense of the fifth commandment, which exhorts us to honor our father and mother, promising long life in the land to those who do. We all somehow sense that when the family is weak, when children are not taught a sense of right and wrong, when they have no stability and do not see faithful love shown to them, the whole society is affected. But Jesus does not advocate "family values."

JESUS' FAMILY VALUES

Jesus said that he came not to bring peace, but a sword (Matt. 10:34). His words are shocking: "I have come to turn 'a man against his father, a daughter against her mother, a daughter-in-law against her mother-in-law—a man's enemies will be the members of his own household'" (Matt. 10:35–36). Jesus was quoting from the prophecy of Micah (7:6), a prophet who described the sin of Israel as he watched for the coming of God his Savior to deliver him. Jesus came as that deliverer, but Jesus warns that faith in him will divide families. Under Islamic law, a believer in Jesus may be put to death for apostasy. Many Christians have been disowned by families that reject the Christian faith. Jesus' "family values" do not guarantee stability, prosperity, and happiness to any culture that will obey his set of family rules. Jesus does advocate "family values," but those values concern the blessings given to *his* family, the family of God.

Jesus' mother and brothers once came from Nazareth to bring him home from a house in Capernaum. His teaching and behavior had them thinking, "He is out of his mind." He needed a rest cure with his family. But when word comes to Jesus that "your mother and brothers are outside looking for you," he does not stop teaching. Instead, he says, "Who are my mother and my brothers?" Looking around at those encircled about him, he answers his own question: "Here are my mother and my brothers! Whoever does God's will is my brother and sister and mother" (see Mark 3:21–34).

We must not misunderstand this story. Jesus loved his mother. From the cross he charged John to care for her. He loved his brothers, who did not yet believe in him. But Jesus here shows his earthly family, his disciples, the crowd, and those who read the story today that his true family was bound not by the blood of physical descent, but by his own blood, given on the cross.

THE PHARISEES' FAMILY VALUES

Jesus' family values are ultimately kingdom values. Yet members of Jesus' redeemed family will treat their earthly families with deeper respect than those who claim superficial "family values," as did the Pharisees of Jesus' time. Jesus transforms all the commandments but never discards them, as we have seen. He deepens them and gives them fresh meaning. He rebuked the Pharisees and legal scholars for evading the law by their legalism. The Pharisees defended the honor of their parents and vociferously argued that a son of Israel owed allegiance to the command to honor father and mother. But they found it onerous to support their parents financially! How could they get around that obligation? Simply by dedicating everything they owned to God. What could be more holy than that? They declared all their possessions to be under the ban (*korban*), given to God, dedicated to the temple treasury. Jesus saw through their subterfuge. This was not sincere worship of God, nor was it true obedience to the command to honor their parents. Rather, their ploy was a hypocritical evasion of their duty to their parents. In order to understand how to honor our earthly father or mother, we must understand the deeper family values that Jesus shows us.

In Christ, the commandment to honor father and mother is fulfilled. The apostle Paul perceived the reality of Christ's family when he prayed to the Father in heaven, "from whom his whole family in heaven and on earth derives its name" (Eph. 3:15). The Greek word for "family" is *patria*, "fatherdom," derived from *pater*, "father." The whole family, the church of Christ, takes its name from the Father because it is united to his Son.

A SPIRITUAL FAMILY

Does this spiritual family mean that earthly families now have no significance? Surely not. Jesus welcomed parents who brought little children to him for his blessing. They were in his arms and in his kingdom. He blessed them in the name of his

Father, putting the divine name upon them. Circumcision marked children out as belonging to God. And in the New Covenant, whole families are baptized at once, entering as families into the name of the Father, the Son, and the Holy Ghost.

But there is another sense in which Christ fulfills the "family values" that God instituted in creation, when he made male and female in his image and set "the lonely in families" (Ps. 68:61). Paul writes about how Jesus transformed the law: "Children, obey your parents in the Lord, for this is right. 'Honor your father and mother'—which is the first commandment with a promise—'that it may go well with you and that you may enjoy long life on the earth'" (Eph. 6:1–3).

FAMILY "IN THE LORD"

"In the Lord"—there you have the transformation of the law in Jesus. The law still applies; it still promises blessing, not just in the land, but in the whole earth. The bond in the home between parents and children is not broken, but it is deepened and drawn into the love of Christ. As we will see, "in the Lord" changes the love between husband and wife. In the same way it changes the relation between parents and children. Fathers are reminded that they are not to exasperate their children, but to bring them up in the nurture and admonition of the Lord. A father does not merely "command" nurture, but provides it in a loving way that allows the children to understand it and to receive it, whether it is good physical food, consumed with respectful manners, or good spiritual food, received with a respectful heart. The family is in Christ, and Christ, the Head of the church, is also Head of the family.

In Brooklyn as well as in Jerusalem, Hasidic Jews sometimes wear on their heads a phylactery, a box of black leather divided in four sections for Scripture portions. One portion is "Hear, O Israel: The LORD our God, the LORD is one. Love the LORD your God with all your heart and with all your soul and with all your strength" (Deut. 6:4–5).

That passage goes on to say, "These commandments that I give you today are to be upon your hearts. Impress them on your children. Talk about them when you sit at home and when you walk along the road, when you lie down and when you get up. Tie them as symbols on your hands and bind them on your foreheads. Write them on the doorframes of your houses and on your gates" (Deut. 6:6–9).

Love for God cannot be tied on in a box. Neither can we tie it on our children. Only Jesus ever loved the Father with all his heart and soul. The price of his love for his Father was to lose the love of his Father on the cross. He did that to bear the wrath that our sin deserved. The nurture of the Lord Jesus Christ is stronger than the bond of the family in the Old Covenant. Nurture in the Lord respects his lordship over our children. They do not belong to the state, as Communism and nationalism have claimed. Neither do they belong to themselves, as Americans since the sixties of the last century have believed. And ultimately, they do not even belong to their parents, into whose womb and home they are placed by God. They belong only to the Lord. Parents in particular, along with the whole fellowship of the church, have the duty and privilege of affirming Christ's lordship over the lives of their children.

TAKING THE FAMILY NAME

Children are baptized into the name of the Father, the Son, and the Holy Spirit. Baptism is a naming ceremony. We saw in the third commandment something of the power and sanctity of God's name. God's holy name, given to a child in baptism, is not vain or powerless. It is a sign of God's faithful promises to believers and to their children. Jesus took little infants and children in his arms and blessed them, putting the name of his Father upon them. The priest's blessing in the book of Numbers says, "The LORD bless you and keep you; the LORD make his face shine upon you and be gracious to you; the LORD turn his face toward you and give you peace." The meaning of the blessing follows: "So they will put my name on the Israelites, and I will bless them" (Num. 6:24–27). In the Great Commission, Jesus commanded his disciples to "go and make disciples of all nations, baptizing them in the name of the Father and of the Son and of the Holy Spirit" (Matt. 28:19).

Those who are baptized are given God's name as their last name, their family name. Because infant baptism claims the covenant promise for these little ones, they are not to be treated as those who have no right to say, "Our Father." They are born in sin, but they ought not to be excluded from the family of the Lord until they are old enough to profess his name before the church. Christians who bring their children in dedication rightly understand that those children belong to the Lord. Yet in order for the holy name of God to be placed on a child in blessing, the sign of cleansing in the water is needed. Baptism is not a magical ceremony that guarantees salvation. The water used in baptism is a reminder of the cleansing that Jesus made possible through his death on the cross. No matter how cute those babies are on the day of their baptism, they have been tainted with sin since before they were born. Only through faith in Christ's death on their behalf will they be cleansed from that sin.

As he does with all the commandments, Jesus transforms the fifth commandment to honor one's parents. Christian children honor not only their parents, but also church members who show them Jesus. Knowing God as Father through Jesus provides family blessing to parents, children, singles, and orphans—a blessing that goes far beyond that enjoyed by believers under the Old Covenant. The greater blessing comes through the presence of the Holy Spirit. Christian parents nurture their children not only through formal instruction of the law of God, but also as they live out that law in everyday life. Parents show their children Jesus' love as they pour themselves out for their children and courageously and humbly correct and guide them.

THE RULES OF FAMILY LIVING

Structure and order, whether in the home, in life, or in society, involve submission of some to others.[1] In Christ such structures are transformed, for our submission to authority is motivated by our submission in the fear (or reverence) of Christ (Eph. 5:21). Jesus is Lord, and in submitting to him, we submit also to those structures he has ordained for our good and even for our glory. We find joy in submitting to others when we know that it is to Jesus as Lord that we ultimately submit, who is above all authority, and who, as the God-man, is himself in submission to the Father. As the Son brings all things under the authority of the Father, the Father glorifies him and lifts him up. We see parallels of this glory in human relationships. The wife who gladly supports and honors her husband and works always for his good, who is a woman in whom his heart trusts fully—such a woman is praised by her husband and her children and glorified in Christ. The man who submits to Christ and gives his life in loving sacrifice for his wife and children will be lifted up and glorified in the last day. Children who gladly follow the advice and counsel of godly parents will reap rich blessings of wisdom, peace, and strength in their adult lives. Sinners lambaste God's structures and portray them as restrictive and tyrannical. But the "yoke" that Christ took on himself and the one he asks us to take up is the obedience that brings freedom, peace, joy, and honor.

"On your face before God, on your feet before men." So John Clelland, a Presbyterian preacher of the last generation, described the liberty we have in Christ. True freedom is not that shown by the man possessed by a legion of devils in Mark chapter 5. He was free—free of home responsibilities. He did not have to care for a wife or children. He could leave them and do his own thing. He resented the confinement of clothing. He took it all off. He could live where he wanted, so he lived in caves and howled all night. He disliked people. When they came through his haunts, he beat them up. When he was seized and chained, he had the preternatural strength to rip off the bonds and break the chains. Young people who resent the restraints of life at home need to reflect on the total freedom that Satan offers. The freedom of the demoniac was total bondage to a legion of devils. Satan is a destroyer, not a creator.

DESTRUCTION OF GOD'S STRUCTURES

C. S. Lewis, in his novel *Perelandra*, describes a scene on the planet Venus. The hero, Ransom, has been transported there to oppose the Tempter, who is assaulting the Eve of that planet. The Tempter, using a scientist he possesses, presents flattering pictures to this Eve of the heroic future she can provide for her race by disobeying God's command not to leave the floating islands to live on the fixed lands. (Lewis's knowledge of Venus was written long before men had walked on the moon.)

Satan's tool argues with brilliant fallacies in tempting her. Ransom falls asleep, and awakes with a start, fearing that he has failed. But the woman is asleep, too. He goes in search of the scientist, Weston, and finds him by following a trail of flayed birds left on the ground in their blood. He comes upon the demonized man, hunched down, jamming a long fingernail behind the head of a living bird. Logical discourse was only the devil's tool. The heart of demonic evil is destruction of the work of the Lord.

Apart from Christ, no true freedom exists. Submission to him delivers us from bondage to our pride, our evil desires, and our service to the devil. When we pray, "Deliver us from the Evil One," we pray for freedom by enslaving ourselves to the will of our Savior, Christ.

HONOR EXPANDED

Submission to Christ, as we have seen, also enables us to submit to others. Not only do we respect the Lord's ordinances of authority in the home, the church, and the state. We also seek opportunities to serve others—to give a cup of cold water in the name of Jesus. Freedom means service to others for Christ's sake. "You, my brothers," Paul writes, "were called to be free. But do not use your freedom to indulge the sinful nature; rather, serve one another in love. The entire law is summed up in a single command: 'Love your neighbor as yourself'" (Gal. 5:13–14). For that reason, we are to bear one another's burdens and so fulfill the law of Christ.

This is the law as we now receive it, transformed by Jesus Christ, who loved us and gave himself for us. Jesus intends for us to honor not only our parents, but all those in the family of God. We honor others above ourselves. In the love of Christ, we "share with God's people who are in need" and "practice hospitality" (Rom. 12:13). Peter instructs us: "Show proper respect to everyone: Love the brotherhood of believers, fear God, honor the king" (1 Peter 2:17).

Paul had been told in his calling that he would suffer much for Christ's sake. When we read Luke's account of the apostle's service in the book of Acts, we discover that his service of others drew him again and again into stonings, floggings, and apparently even the arena with wild beasts. Yet in all this, he knew the sharing of Christ's sufferings, that is, suffering for the sake of Christ. In his suffering, Paul knew the presence of Christ. For that reason he could sing praise in the prison at Philippi with his feet in stocks and his back bleeding.

In his letters, the apostle described his sufferings to the family of God. They were his fellow workers, belonging to the household of God. Paul thought of himself as a builder, building on the one foundation, Jesus Christ. The building was the temple, the "house of God." When we speak of the house for a family, we call it a "home." Among the people of God, we are "at home." The house of God in Christ is not a shrine, such as an idol might have. Jesus calls us into his home, as it is now seen in the family of believers, and as it will be finally seen when we meet him in our heavenly home.

My five children are urging us to consider another family reunion. It is an impossible task to gather five children, their spouses, twenty-one grandchildren, and ten great-grandchildren from as far away as Berlin, London, Florida, and California (we live in Virginia). But whenever we get some portion of this group together, I have an overwhelming sense of gratitude to God for his rich blessing to me and my wife. Our children love and honor us, sinners though we are. They bring great honor to our family name. You will know how to honor your father and mother as you follow our

Savior, Jesus, who lived his life in submission to his heavenly Father's will. In the power of the Holy Spirit, who raised Christ from the dead, we can bring honor to our family name—"Christian." The suffering, sacrifice, and difficulty that such a path brings us will one day be swallowed up in the joy of our family reunion in heaven with our older brother, Jesus Christ, who has prepared the way for us.

STUDY QUESTIONS

Think It Through:

1. What shocking things does Jesus say about "family values"? How does Jesus transform the fifth commandment?

2. How did the Pharisees sometimes evade their duty to their parents?

3. "Children, obey your parents in the Lord" (Eph. 6:1). How does "in the Lord" determine how we raise our children?

4. How do children receive their last name in the family of God?

5. Order in the church requires submission to one another. What is the form of that order in the family? In the church as the family of God?

6. Contrast true freedom with the freedom of the Gadarene demoniac, who could not be bound.

Take It to Heart:

1. Paul gladly endured suffering for the sake of serving others. In times of personal suffering, have you been able to see in it opportunities to serve others? Has your suffering helped you to sympathize with others? (2 Cor. 1:3–7)

2. Share with others an incident in your family in which love bound up brokenness. Have you seen that principle at work in the church as the family of the Lord?

3. Reflect on a time when your membership in the family of God brought deliverance and blessing for yourself or for others.

4. How do Christian family values help us to show unbelievers what God's family is like?

7

THE SIXTH COMMANDMENT

The Lord of Life

"You shall not murder." (Ex. 20:13 NIV)
"Thou shalt not kill." (KJV)

In April 2001, Holland earned the dubious honor of being the first country to give legal status to doctor-assisted suicide when the Dutch Senate legalized euthanasia. How far Holland has come! During the Nazi occupation of the Netherlands, Dutch doctors refused to obey orders to let elderly or terminally ill patients die without further treatment. Yet it took only one generation, as Malcolm Muggeridge has noted, "to transform a war crime into an act of compassion."[1] Oddly, it was the doctors themselves who led the way in promoting the practice. The Dutch Pediatric Society issued guidelines for killing infants in 1993. "The Royal Dutch Society of Pharmacology sends a book to all new doctors that includes formulas for euthanasia-inducing poisons."[2] In the United States, Dr. Jack Kevorkian has challenged laws against euthanasia by publicizing his practice of it.

Our society struggles with other questions about the preservation of life: capital punishment, the peacekeeping assignments of U.S. troops, and wars to defend life and liberty.

Understanding how Christ transforms the law should help us reflect on these questions.

The preciousness of human life taught by Jesus has worked as a leaven to transform society wherever the gospel has spread. The gospel approach to honoring human life avoids two extremes. It avoids setting human life above all value for truth and for God himself. It also avoids devaluing human life so that there is no longer any distinction between human life and any other kind of life.

MISTAKEN NOTIONS OF THE VALUE OF HUMAN LIFE

Patterns of tribal war in Africa give us one example of a distorted view of human life. These societies may have understood in some small way that there are times when an individual sacrifices his life for the greater good of society. In such societies, the tribe is the greater good. The theology of tribalism sanctifies the life of the tribe, which is believed to have descended from a god. Outsiders are often viewed as inhuman. In the Japanese culture, similar myths helped foster savagery in conquest and the willingness to sacrifice life in suicide. Such practices come from a false deification of certain human groups. One might also see such tendencies in Muslim beliefs, which teach that infidels are to be seen as a lesser category of human, undeserving of life. Suicide bombers show a willingness to sacrifice their own lives for what they view as a higher cause. As unnerving and repulsive as we find such actions, we must admit to seeing some reflection of the truth in such societies, for the Bible itself teaches that there are some principles for which we should be ready to die. Human life is not to be elevated above all else.

There is another extreme that sees human life as no more valuable than animal or plant life. Animal-rights advocates have begun to abandon the distinctiveness of human life. Dr. Peter Singer, professor of ethics at Princeton University, teaches that mankind is simply one species of primate, with no more rights than any other mammal.[3] He defends a Darwinian explanation of the evolution of the social contract, the "tit-for-tat" strategy of human behavior. He argues that evolved strategies of human behavior "amount to nothing less than an experimental refutation of Jesus' celebrated teaching about turning the other cheek." According to Singer, the morally right action is that which satisfies the preferences of the greatest number of people. Even if a "divine command" exists, mankind has no need for it as a basis for ethics. The one view that must be rejected is the Christian "fundamentalist" view—the biblical account that God created Adam. Yet this is the very account for which Jesus provides deep understanding.

A SCRIPTURAL VIEW OF THE VALUE OF HUMAN LIFE

Scripture gives the rationale for the preciousness of human life. God created mankind in his image. We are created for fellowship with God, and called to be his stewards of creation. Insofar as we are reflections of God's image, we are not God himself. Thus it is wrong to deify human life and to make everything dependent on its conservation. On the other hand, God himself has given life, and because he sets such high value on it, we are called to do the same. We cannot raise a grasshopper to the level of a human, nor can we keep a clean conscience when we eliminate a child's life through abortion or an elderly person's life through euthanasia.

Jesus himself shows us the right view of human life. Jesus does not place a distorting value on his own physical life, for he is ready to lay it down voluntarily for the sake of our salvation. But he does not denigrate his life, either, by valuing the animals as equals, or by refusing to eat or care for his body. As we have seen, Jesus Christ bears the image of God, not only as a man, but also as the God-man. By bearing God's image in his human nature, Jesus showed the wonder of that likeness. By bearing God's likeness in his divine nature, the Son of God became our Savior, present with us.

LIFE AND THE STATE

In Old Testament law, capital punishment is required for murder because man bears God's image. Blood is the liquid of life, and one guilty of bloodshed must pay with his own blood (Gen. 9:4–6). Humanism rejects capital punishment in an attempt, it would seem, to value man and to honor him. Yet humanism rejects the image of God in man, and thus, ironically, it fails to take man seriously enough. Though it is intended to glorify man, it in fact demeans him, making his actions less important and less meaningful than they are if God's image is taken into account. Humanism thus demeans the nature of man and the importance of his actions by failing to require punishment for transgression. Instead it recognizes only deterrence and rehabilitation. Unbelief rejects the justice and judgment of God, and therefore questions the foreshadowing of God's judgment in the judgment of the state. The Bible teaches us otherwise: we are not victims of our genetics and our environment. We are responsible agents, bearing God's image.[4]

The modern secular state remains an authority established by God, serving (although imperfectly) the exercise of justice.

Paul writes, "The authorities that exist have been established by God. Consequently, he who rebels against the authority is rebelling against what God has instituted, and those who do so will bring judgment on themselves" (Rom. 13:1b–2). Without the exercise of state power to punish crime, human life falls victim to terror. Lawlessness still threatens the modern world, not only under corrupt governments, but also through the actions of fanatical advocates of disorder.

We often suppress the knowledge of our own guilt before God, but we can more readily see the guilt of others. Hitler's callous destruction of the elderly, the maimed, the Jews, and the gypsies; the abduction and drugging of young boys in Africa in order to force them to cut off the hands of their own friends and relatives; the execution by roasting in the desert sun of truckloads of Afghans at the hands of fellow Afghans; the gruesome televised beheadings of Turkish truck drivers delivering goods to Iraq; the inhuman sexual humiliation imposed on Iraqi prisoners by self-absorbed young Americans—these and similar crimes still provoke moral outrage when we hear of them. Yet, in the sight of the holy God, we are all guilty of dishonoring life. In our rebellion against his goodness and truth, we fail to stand up for the weak and helpless. We keep our food to ourselves, forgetting the widows and the orphans. We are too frightened to engage in the defense of the unborn children of our land. The stench of our crimes strikes infinite revulsion in God, all the more because of his incomparable purity and holiness.

THE DEEPER COMMANDMENT

Jesus deepened this commandment as he did the others (Matt. 5:21ff.). It is obvious that the commandment as it was written forbids taking human life unjustly. But Jesus shows us the depth and breadth of this commandment. He said that anyone who spoke angry words against his brother was answerable to the court of the church and that "anyone who says, 'You fool!' will be in danger of the fire of hell" (Matt. 5:22).

Actual physical injury is not the only way to break this commandment; hatred, scorn, or malice has already broken it, and requires repentance. Even the physical death sentence, which is the most severe judgment rendered by human courts for murder, pales into insignificance when set next to God's punishment. God threatens us with the "second death," eternal judgment of the soul. Rebellion against God-given physical life is also rebellion against the very Spirit of God, the Giver of Life. It reaps death, the wages of sin, both physically and spiritually. Of course, we are all murderers in the sense that we have failed to love as we ought. There is no one who has not thought "You idiot!" about someone. So what hope do we have of avoiding the second death?

OUR POSITIVE ANTIDOTE

As with the other commandments, Jesus transforms this one by more than his condemnation of murderers. He provides the very Life that can rescue us from our murderous selves. He brings the life of the new creation in himself. He is the Way, the Truth, the Life. "In him was life, and that life was the light of men" (John 1:4). Jesus brought that life through giving his own life for sinners. He shed his lifeblood to give eternal life through his death. He speaks words of life, for he presents himself as the Bread of Life. "This bread is my flesh, which I will give for the life of the world" (John 6:51c). Once again, we discover that the commandments take us to the cross and to the ministry of Jesus that led to the cross. He healed the sick and raised the dead. Those who would claim to be pro-life must be pro-Life: pro—Lord of Life.

Jesus rose from the dead. Death could not hold him; neither can it hold us. Paul can cry, "Death has been swallowed up in victory" (1 Cor. 15:54). He draws this idea from Isaiah 25:8, and adds a quotation from Hosea 13:14: "Where, O death, is your victory? Where, O death, is your sting?" (1 Cor. 15:55).

The prophets foretold God's final triumph over sin and the curse. They saw, too, the price of redemption in the sufferings and triumph of God's Servant. Jesus fulfills all prophecy in ways beyond anticipation, for all the Law and the Prophets point to life in him. We share that life because Jesus rose for us, as he burst out of the grave and shattered the gates of death. We share his life, too, in the mystery of our vital union with him. We rose with him, and we reign with him in the union of branches with the Vine, the bride with the Bridegroom.

Our living union with Christ is real in our experience through the work of the Holy Spirit in our hearts. The Spirit tells us that we belong to Jesus. You may find expressions of Christian experience a little sentimental, or even conceited. Should the writer of the hymn "In the Garden," beloved of your grandparents, claim knowledge of the love of Jesus that "none other has ever known"? Perhaps not, yet a generation prized that hymn because it speaks of a reality. The Spirit does witness in our hearts, pouring out the Lord's love for us so that we are aware of it. Part of our obedience of this commandment is abiding in Christ, staying connected to the Head, and thus to the life that the Head provides us through his Spirit. The Spirit of God keeps us in life, both physically and spiritually.

KINGDOM PACIFISM

Jesus also transforms this commandment by refusing the use of the sword for himself and his kingdom. In the garden of

Gethsemane, Jesus commanded Peter to sheathe his sword, and healed the severed ear of Malchus, whom Peter had probably tried to behead in his zeal to protect his beloved Savior. Why was it wrong for Peter to defend Christ with the sword? After all, had not the Lord himself sanctioned the sword earlier in Israel's history?

In the Old Testament, God revealed himself in judgment on the foes of Israel. Israel entered the land as avenging angels, executing God's judgments on the Canaanites. In the name of the Lord, David's slingshot brought down Goliath. David as the warrior king subdued the surrounding nations, establishing a kingdom that Solomon could rule in peace. Isaiah told how God would use Assyria as his ax and saw to cut down the pride of Israel, but then bring destruction upon them, and raise up the standard of the Messiah (Isa. 10:15; 11:10). He foresaw the coming of the Messiah as the Prince of Peace.

But Jesus takes the sword away from the disciples of his kingdom, except as used for personal defense. No longer are his disciples to be a nation among nations. Only when the Roman emperor Constantine formalized Christianity as a legitimate religion did the process begin that led again to nations taking the sword in the name of Christ. The Crusades showed the disastrous misunderstanding of the change that Jesus brought. The new Israel formed by faith and preached by Paul was not extended by conquest but by the preaching of the gospel. We now take for granted the teaching of Jesus that his kingdom is heavenly and spiritual. Yet the change is total. As we saw in our discussion of God's image, Jesus called for a denarius in his discussion with his disciples about the validity of paying taxes to Caesar, a pagan king. Jesus says, "Give to Caesar what is Caesar's, and to God what is God's" (Matt. 22:21). The coin bore Caesar's image, and thus "belonged" to Caesar. The nations now had the power of the sword to use in upholding good. Jesus transformed the place of pagan nations in maintaining of peace and order.

The physical distinctiveness of Israel no longer marks the new Israel. For that reason the kosher diet no longer applies, and the separation of Israel from table fellowship with Gentiles is ended. The mark of the new Israel is love toward God and toward the people we meet—and the people we would rather not meet. This love, as we have seen, is the infinitely deepened love that Jesus showed to his Father and to us. The love of Christ draws and drives us to talk to people, to surprise others by seeing what they need.

Again we see the "putting off" and the "putting on" principle. Christians are not only called to desist from murder and to avoid calling their brothers "fools." They are to cling to life as God has intended it to be lived, namely, in communion with his life-giving Spirit through the resurrection power of Jesus Christ. From that position of absorbing the power of Christ's life, they are able to dispense life as they meet the physical and spiritual needs of others.

Hundreds of thousands of refugees in Sri Lanka, Indonesia, and Thailand were left without potable water after the stunning tsunami wiped out whole villages on the day after Christmas 2004. Many nations rushed to provide water and food to the survivors. Christians might well keep in mind the picture of needy hands raised, ready to receive bottles of water and bags of noodles and rice. Christians not only give a cup of cold water in the name of Christ, but become sources of life-giving water, wells overflowing with bounty and goodness, to all those with whom they come in contact. Those who are new creatures in Christ, alive from the dead, are made ambassadors, administrators of life. What a privilege the children of God have. Not only have they been rescued from the second death, but they have been made sources of life. Jesus returned to heaven after conquering death. He gave his life-giving Spirit to his people so that as they move out into the deserts of this life, they are sources of life. They plead with others to get right with God (2 Cor. 5:20). They can tell their friends and enemies alike to "get a life" with the Lord.

STUDY QUESTIONS

Think It Through:

1. Dr. Peter Singer was appointed to a chair in bioethics at Princeton University's Center for Human Values. He is known for his evolutionary leveling of human life with animal life. Why does the Christian faith regard human life as sacred? How does this belief affect the argument about abortion?

2. What is the biblical teaching about capital punishment?

3. How did Jesus deepen the commandment, "Thou shalt not kill"?

4. In Ephesians and Colossians, find some contrasts between the attitudes that lead to division, strife, and murder, and those graces that bring unity and peace.

5. Why is the physical resurrection of Jesus the key to his gift of spiritual life?

6. Jesus said, "This bread is my flesh, which I will give for the life of the world" (John 6:51). How does the death of Jesus bring life?

7. Why do secular nations have the power of the sword, while the sword is now denied to the church?

Take It to Heart:

1. Do you thank the Lord for making you a new creature in Christ, and therefore already part of the new creation? Pray together that we may believe what is true about our life.

2. Pray for Christians who are being martyred for Christ. Pray, too, that we will not be ashamed of him.

3. Reflect on the leading of the Lord Jesus in your life. You have heard the slogan, "Get a life!" Ask for vision. The Lord does have a plan for your life, and leads you as your Shepherd. What is his calling for you? Discuss this in your group.

THE SEVENTH COMMANDMENT

Purity in Christ

✣

"Thou shalt not commit adultery." (Ex. 20:14 KJV)

Like many other deteriorating cultures before it, the American culture has become sex-crazed. Lust sweeps past satiety into perversion. But perversion has been with us since the beginning. The list of deviant sexual behaviors as found in Leviticus 18 shows us that mankind very quickly distorted God's gift of sexuality, making sexual lust into an idol that steals the hearts of men away from their God. In his letter to the Romans, the apostle Paul describes the downward vortex of deepening vileness in Gentile society. Paul would not be surprised by pedophilia, or by pornography on the Internet! And Jesus knew even more than Paul just how depraved the human heart can be.

MARRIAGE, ADULTERY, AND DIVORCE ACCORDING TO JESUS

Jesus fulfills the seventh commandment, "Thou shalt not commit adultery," as he does the others, by deepening its meaning and by transforming it as he gives it to us. In each of the Ten Commandments Jesus does not set aside the law, but deepens its authority and scope. When he speaks of adultery, he again moves from external obedience to purity of heart:

> You have heard that it was said, "Do not commit adultery." But I tell you that anyone who looks at a woman lustfully has already committed adultery with her in his heart. If your right eye causes you to sin, gouge it out and throw it away. It is better for you to lose one part of your body than for your whole body to be thrown into hell. (Matt. 5:27–29)

No wonder Jesus said, "Unless your righteousness surpasses that of the Pharisees and the teachers of the law, you will certainly not enter the kingdom of heaven" (Matt. 5:20). Outward conformity can never please God, who sees our hearts.

Jesus dealt with divorce by again strengthening the command. The law of Moses made provision for divorce. It required that a man provide a certificate of divorce to end a marriage (Deut. 24:1–4). But listen to Jesus: "But I tell you that anyone who divorces his wife, except for marital unfaithfulness, causes her to commit adultery, and anyone who marries a woman so divorced commits adultery" (Matt. 5:32).

Jesus explained the sanctity of marriage by taking us back to God's purpose in creation. The Creator made mankind male and female so that the two might become one flesh in marriage. "What God has joined together, let man not separate" (Matt. 19:6b). The Pharisees objected to such a high standard by arguing that Moses had sanctioned divorce. But Jesus explained that divorce was permitted only because of their hard hearts. "It was not this way from the beginning," he said (Matt. 19:8b). By going back to creation, before the law of Moses, Jesus put that law in its place in the history of redemption. God had clearly shown his purpose in his creation of Adam and Eve. He made them not only to share his image, but to be one flesh. The creation account describes God's taking a rib from Adam's side (next to his heart, as marriage sermons often remind us). From Adam's flesh and bone his wife was formed. The bond of marriage is indeed physical and biological, but it is also deeply theological, as "one flesh" shows.

MARRIAGE AS A REFLECTION OF COVENANT

In spite of the high divorce rate and the cavalier attitude we seem to have about marriage, something in our human soul hankers after that elusive fidelity that marriage promises. When actress Jennifer Aniston and her handsome actor-husband Brad Pitt broke up, one stunned and disappointed fan bemoaned the split: "I can't tell you how many people have said to me, 'If they can't make it, who can?' "[1] Though perhaps misplaced, the hope of these fans taps into a structure that God placed in the world as a picture of his fidelity to his people. The prophet Ezekiel uses the figure of marriage to describe God's covenant relation to Israel. He speaks of marriage in its legal force as a figure for God's covenant made at Sinai. Yet it is not left as one contract among others. No, the Lord holds his people with jealous love. He cannot permit other gods to share his claim of love. The worship of other gods is the greatest offense against the Lord, whom the people of Israel must love with all their heart, soul, mind, and strength.

The prophets describe the love of God for his people as the love of a father leading his son Israel through the desert.

"When Israel was a child, I loved him, and out of Egypt I called my son . . . It was I who taught Ephraim to walk, taking them by the arms; but they did not realize it was I who healed them" (Hos. 11:1, 3). More often, the prophets speak of God as a loving husband. The time when God led Israel through the wilderness was a tryst with them. The Lord was wooing his people and leading them home to the house where he would dwell with them. When Israel turned aside in spiritual adultery, the Lord cried, "How can I give you up, Ephraim? How can I hand you over, Israel? . . . My heart is changed within me; all my compassion is aroused" (Hos. 11:8).

The Lord, the Creator, uses the image of a husband's love to show the love he has for Israel:

> For your Maker is your husband—the LORD Almighty is his name—the Holy One of Israel is your Redeemer . . . The LORD will call you back as if you were a wife deserted and distressed in spirit—a wife who married young, only to be rejected . . . For a brief moment I abandoned you, but with deep compassion I will bring you back. (Isa. 54:5–7)

The Lord gives his people tender names of love, the way a husband would proudly claim and perhaps even tease his wife, loving her for just the person she is. "You will be called Hephzibah [my delight is in her], and your land Beulah [married]; for the LORD will take delight in you, and your land will be married . . . As a bridegroom rejoices over his bride, so will your God rejoice over you" (Isa. 62:4b–5).

Ezekiel 16 compares the Lord's love to that of a young man who discovers an abandoned baby girl, kicking in her blood by the side of the road. He finds the girl, washes and clothes her, and provides for her as she grows into a beautiful young woman. He then marries her, spreading his robe

94

over her in protection and claiming her as his beloved bride. God says that he has taken to himself his bride, his people Israel. But the bride, wedded to the Lord in his covenant, becomes a prostitute, and offers up the children of the Lord to heathen gods. The Lord will judge her, but at last restore her and establish his covenant with her.

There will come a great and final day when the covenant is fulfilled, not by the faithfulness of the bride, but by the steadfast love of the Bridegroom. That day will bring the sealing of the love of the Lord for his people. " 'In that day,' declares the LORD, 'you will call me "my husband"; you will no longer call me "my master" [Baal]' " (Hos. 2:16). In that day, the Daughter of Zion will sing, for "The LORD your God is with you, he is mighty to save. He will take great delight in you, he will quiet you with his love, he will rejoice over you with singing" (Zeph. 3:17).[2] The prophet speaks of the Lord's deepest love, to be revealed with the coming of the Lord. Then at last, the Lord, the Bridegroom, will come to claim his own.

MARRIAGE: CREATED TO SHOW US ABOUT CHRIST

God did not fish around for some image to use to show his people what his love is like, and then stumble on marriage as the best one to convince them to return to him in covenant devotion. He did not recognize the power of married love and determine to use sexuality as the strongest figure. No. God planned it the other way around. The Lord placed in us at creation deep sexual emotions so that we might understand the jealousy of his love for us and the joy of jealousy for him. In the movie about the life of Alfred Kinsey, his claimed scientific neutrality in describing every sexual perversion as natural is belied by the strong reaction his wife shows when Kinsey himself dabbles in homosexuality. Such deep-seated "jealousy" is right and good, evidencing the natural instinct that God has placed in us as human beings to desire "one true love."

God created that instinct so that we would better understand his faithful love to us. That faithfulness is shown by God's jealous love for his Son. We benefit from that same jealous love of God as we are joined to Christ. Jesus Christ calls himself the Bridegroom, and John the Baptist is the friend of the Bridegroom, calling Israel to repent and come to the wedding feast. The jealousy of the Father, who cannot tolerate idols, is jealousy for his own Son. We are joined to Jesus in a relationship that lasts longer than marriage, for we are joined to him forever. "Dear children," John says, "keep yourselves from idols" (1 John 5:21).

What instruction do we gain from Christ's transformation of the command for sexual purity? Clearly Jesus calls us to his purity, beginning in our hearts, and modeled in our lives. Perhaps in no other area is the contrast of Christian living more plainly seen than in the unusual purity that a Christian keeps in his or her sexual life, remaining a virgin before marriage, and remaining faithful to one wife or husband until death parts that union. (Yes, believe it or not, couples such as this exist!) But as always, we stand before Christ's heart-searching with our shame. For even a Christian who has lived a "pure" life in the sense just mentioned cannot stand before Christ's demands for purity. What husband has not looked on another woman and lusted? What wife has not thought, "Why did God give me this husband? Would I not have been happier with another?" What spouse, male or female, has not dreamed of using his or her body to impress or to manipulate? What single has not been tempted to idolize a longed-for marriage partner rather than trusting God for the sufficiency of his love? And if our fidelity in marriage and sexuality is weak, what hope do we have of standing pure in our fidelity to our Savior? We hear what he says, and we despair. Who is capable of such purity?

JESUS, THE ONLY PURE ONE

Only Jesus was truly pure. He kept for us the seventh commandment against adultery. His holiness is the ground of our justification in this area of purity. When God ordered the children of Israel to make the tabernacle, he ordered a basin to be made in order to wash the hands and feet of the priests who would come into the Tent of Meeting. They were to be pure before entering into God's presence. Of course, water cannot purify us from sin. It is Christ's holiness that satisfies God's stringent demands for purity. Christ's holiness is the basin in which we wash in order to be pure in our thoughts and lives. His transformation of the law draws us to him. He is our only hope. It is the pure water of God's Word that washes our consciences clean—not only the written Word, but the pure Word of the person of Christ himself. In the purity we receive through our baptism in him, we are able to live out the purity he requires of us. It is in the hope of his perfection and in the power of his pure Spirit that we can begin to put into practice a flickering candle of purity in our sexual lives and in our steadfast love of our Savior.

THE RESTORATION OF MARRIAGE BY THE POWER OF THE SPIRIT

The apostle Paul speaks of marriage as he presents the roles of submission in households. Wives are to submit to husbands, children to parents, and slaves to masters. Yet all such submission takes place in the fear of the Lord. He alone is the

Lord of all. That relation to Christ transforms all submission, for all are joined to Christ and enjoy the liberty in which Christ has set them free. Our submission to that dear Savior is the source of self-sacrificing love that enables us as Christians in all our human relationships. In our submission to Christ, and to the power of his Spirit working in us, we are enabled to find joy in the structures God has created. What sin has disrupted the power of the Spirit can restore.

To submit for Christ's sake is to submit to Christ where he has placed us. No other is master of our hearts. The submissive Christian is an odd combination. The world does not understand such a position. There is a strange power and independence to a man or woman who is not "for sale." How many times has a boss fired or refused to hire a Christian, when he realized that his heart was not for hire! On the other hand, submission to others for Christ's sake calls for service with dedicated dignity, "like slaves of Christ, doing the will of God from your heart. Serve wholeheartedly, as if you were serving the Lord, not men" (Eph. 6:6–7). As Christians submit to the obedience to which God calls them, in the place of service where he has put them, they are strengthened by the Spirit to submit. In that strength, they serve with full hearts, and it is the Lord himself who will honor such service.

Faithfulness to the purity of our love for God implies not only faithfulness in the marriage itself, but also faithfulness in our relationships with our children. Children who are the fruit of a faithful marriage relationship also have the implied duty of faithfulness to that marriage as they exercise, by the power of the Spirit, submission and loving obedience to the parents God has given them. In this obedience, children also learn of the purity of the marriage relationship. They understand its power to show them the love of Christ as they watch their parents' faithfulness to each other. Obedience in the Lord applies to parents as well as to children. They dare not be abusive or demand too much. "Fathers, do not exasperate your children; instead, bring them up in the training and instruction of the Lord" (Eph. 6:4). How much parents learn of the power of God's fatherly love as they have their own children and realize how passionately they care about these little ones.

MARRIAGE AS SEEN FROM THE HEIGHTS

In all the commandments, we see how the law is transformed by the rule of Christ. This is certainly true in sexual relations. The sexual relation of one man with one woman as one body in marriage has a new law *in Christ*. Although Adam was created first, and the principle of the husband as head of the home is already present in the Old Testament, Paul gives this principle a new foundation. He says, "Wives, submit to your husbands *as to the Lord*. For the husband is the head of the wife as Christ is the head of the church, his body, of which he is the Savior. Now as the church submits to Christ, so also wives should submit to their husbands in everything" (Eph. 5:22–24).

Paul starts with the supremacy of Christ, and the reality of his presence in the Spirit. From this, he speaks of Christ and his church, then makes that reality the master model for our roles in the families that are "in the Lord." Does it seem that the role of the husband is exalted too much, that he should be likened to Christ? Ah, but that likeness offers no autocratic rule like that of the kings of the Gentiles. Christ is no dictator, but he is the Head of his body the church—in organic union with her. He is the Savior of the church. He loved the church and gave himself up for her. His purpose is "to make her holy, cleansing her by the washing with water through the word, and to present her to himself as a radiant church, without stain or wrinkle or any other blemish, but holy and blameless" (Eph. 5:26–27).

Marriage counselors in the pulpit may feel the need for oxygen to ascend with Paul to such heavenly heights. They prefer to start with specific sources of irritation mentioned by a typical couple. Why did the new husband get so upset to see his wife looking through his wallet? Why does she find total lack of sensitivity in a husband who bangs out his toothbrush without rinsing the basin?

To be sure, men—and women, too—have seized on the idea of submission with no understanding of the transformation brought through Jesus. They miss the sun in the solar system of Paul's commandments. Submission is a meaningless concept in a Christian marriage if the one to whom we are all submitting is left out of the picture. The center is our being "in Christ." Paul's words could not be clearer. "In the Lord" determines everything. Making the husband the head of the house will not yield a Christian marriage or a Christian home. Some poor wives are painfully aware of this, as they try to live peaceably with husbands who take Paul's words, distort them, and impose their own selfish demands on their wives in the guise of Christian submission. Likewise, women can misuse their expectations of husbands by refusing obedience to them until they have "shaped up" and are looking like Paul's ideal model of selflessness. Such women forget that their submission is not ultimately to their husbands, but to Christ, who strengthens them and enables them to submit to a sinner in honor of Christ.

Are Paul's words too theological to be of practical help? Paul certainly knew and understood the teaching of the wisdom books of the Old Testament, which are full of practical applications of godly wisdom. He taught that wisdom, while coming from the Spirit, must be tested and sharpened in experience. But Paul understood why our being joined to Christ through the Spirit is the secret of Christ's union with his body the church. "This is a profound mystery," he says, "but I am talking about Christ and the church" (Eph. 5:32). Paul seems to realize that one might take his words off into a realm of bodiless theology and speculation. Immediately after recognizing the mystery of which he writes, he brings his readers back down to earth with a thump. "However," he adds, as a final word on the issue of marriage, "each one of you also must love his wife as he loves himself, and the wife must respect her husband" (Eph. 5:33). There is no room here for someone who wants to spiritualize away the responsibilities incumbent on husbands or wives.

The husband who imitates the Lord by giving his life for his wife; who has before him Christ's perfecting of the church as his holy bride; who claims her not as his possession, but as belonging to the Lord—that husband will show his wife something of the love of Christ, who calls them to be one flesh. They will together show the world something of the family of God. And the wife who gladly follows her husband; who seeks only his honor and his good; who seeks to bring all things under the headship of Christ by bringing the elements of her own world under the headship of her husband; who longs to accomplish the desires of her husband's heart and to apply those desires to all areas of her authority—that wife will show something of the full submission with which the Son honored his Father.

Such a couple will indeed experience no sense of loss, but the gain of glory. For the wife is the glory of the husband as she submits to him, and the man is glorified and lifted up by the wife who honors him. Both are glorified by the Father and the Son, just as the Son himself is glorified at the last day by the Father to whom he has submitted. Such Christian submission may seem humiliating. But it is the way of Christ, the way of the cross, and the only way to true glory and satisfaction.

OF MEN AND WOMEN IN SOCIETY TODAY

The differing roles of men and women are not understood in our society. The extremes of the feminist movement have destroyed much of our understanding of masculinity and femininity (though I am not suggesting that 1950s America had it right, either). And those extremes have shifted as the homosexual movement has taken us one more step away from the creation order. It is inevitable that those who believe homosexuality to be a perfectly normal and natural sexual expression will hate Christians. Homosexual activists often show hatred for the Christian faith, once setting fire to a church in San Francisco. Four Christians who were among those reading Bible passages at a homosexual gathering on the streets of Philadelphia were arrested for "ethnic intimidation," criminal conspiracy, failure to disperse, disorderly conduct, and obstructing highways. At the date of the writing of this book, they are, between them, facing 47 years of jail time if convicted. The debate rages in our society, and homosexual advocates have made great strides in convincing the general public that it is their democratic right to do as they please in the sexual arena, while it is unlawful to express any condemnation of homosexuality. In 1973, homosexuality was removed from the disorders listed by the American Psychiatric Association.

Dr. Robert Spitzer, a prominent professor of psychiatry, realizes that the gay community considers him an enemy because his studies show that homosexuals who desire to change can be helped to change behavior and to diminish homosexual desires.[3] He has met vigorous opposition from psychiatrists who hold that homosexuality is a fixed element of an individual's nature and that it is therefore unethical to provide psychiatric help to a homosexual who wants it. God's law forbids both homosexual practice and heterosexual adultery or fornication. God created humans male and female, in his image. To deny such distinctions is to work not only against nature, but against the Creator. It is to that Creator that we all must answer for our sexual behavior and for the desires of our hearts.

Jesus transforms the law by providing what the law in itself could never provide—the power of his presence in the Spirit to change our hearts. Jesus taught us to pray, "Lead us not into temptation" (Matt. 6:13). The Spirit can conform our hearts to God's law by changing our desires. Paul, in his first letter to the Corinthians, shows us that transforming power of the Spirit:

> Do not be deceived: Neither the sexually immoral nor idolaters nor adulterers nor male prostitutes nor homosexual offenders nor thieves nor the greedy nor drunkards nor slanderers nor swindlers will inherit the kingdom of God. And that is what some of you were. But you were washed, you were sanctified, you were justified in the name of the Lord Jesus Christ and by the Spirit of our God. (1 Cor. 6:9b–11)

For every Christian, particularly in the sex-soaked culture of our society, our battle against temptation never ceases. We need to be washed, to be sanctified, to be justified in the name of the Lord Jesus and in the power of his Spirit. We need the shield of faith to quench the fiery darts of the Evil One. Christ's transforming power enables us to see others as persons rather than sex objects and to "gird up our loins" with the understanding of true sexual faithfulness. Christian realism, in fellowship with the Lord, dissipates the fog of sexual illusion and fantasy. Even Jennifer Aniston and Brad Pitt could hold a marriage together were they to depend on the power of Christ, our Deliverer, who has promised to be with us. As Christians who know the power of Christ's Spirit, we can help others by listening, praying, and caring. A friend who had long been a practicing homosexual helped me to understand his struggle to rewire his brain, as it were. One aid in his struggle was his perception that under his lust there lurked a murderous desire for a victim.

As the divine Bridegroom, Jesus has transformed the seventh commandment. He has lifted us, through union with himself, to taste the heavenly passion of God's love. The joy of being one flesh in sexual union fades with age, and will not endure through eternity. But the love of his bride, the church, centers on the Lord forever. Only that love will purify the hearts of his own.

George Croly, in his hymn "Spirit of God, Descend upon My Heart," wrote:

> Teach me to love thee as thine angels love,
> One holy passion filling all my frame;
> The baptism of the heav'n-descended Dove,
> My heart an altar, and thy love the flame.[4]

The hymn celebrates the work of the Holy Spirit, who does, indeed, pour out God's love for us in our hearts. Yet our model is not the love of angels, for they marvel at the love of the Lord poured out on unworthy rebels. Our model is the love of Jesus. We love, because he first loved us—loved us, and gave himself for us.

STUDY QUESTIONS

Think It Through:

1. How does Jesus deepen this commandment? When are we guilty of adultery?

2. Is purity possible in our society? What counsel do you give to your children or other young people? Should the church be concerned about the spiritual ramifications of the romance of its young adults?

3. Is it possible for a church to exercise loving discipline in troubled marriages?

4. In what sense is the bond of marriage theological rather than biological?

5. What is the calling of a husband in the marriage relationship? (Eph. 5:22–33) How does the measure of Christ's love transform this relation?

6. What is the role of a wife in the marriage relationship? How does her role reflect that of Christ? How can her submission to her husband be truly fulfilling?

7. How does the love of Christ enable us to see others as persons, not as sex objects?

Take It to Heart:

1. Consider the importance of the prayer: "Lead us not into temptation." The Lord guards us in his providence. How do we make ourselves vulnerable to temptation? How have you fled from temptation? Joseph's flight from the seduction of Potiphar's wife showed his piety in action. Sharing some of the Lord's deliverances in your life might benefit other Christians.

2. Return in your reflection to the purifying fire of the love of Jesus. Only the reality of his love, kindled in your heart by the Spirit, can overwhelm the lure of lust. Pray together for the Spirit to cleanse us and claim us.

9

THE EIGHTH COMMANDMENT

The Lord of the Inheritance

"You shall not steal." (Ex. 20:15)

Human beings are often ready to die to defend their property. Israeli/Palestinian struggles over land, controversial Venezuelan land reform projects, Rwandan massacres of white landholders—such conflicts testify to the value we give to ownership and treasure. In the 2003 forest fires in southern California, Robin Sloan took a few extra minutes to pack mementos and lost her life in the fire.[1] Another woman refused to leave until she had collected her horses. She, too, was destroyed by the raging flames. Were Robin's mementos and Nancy Morphew's horses worth the price of their lives? How many of us, motivated by the fear of losing our material goods, give up far greater joys?

Jesus transforms the eighth commandment, "You shall not steal," by helping us to set our hearts on true treasure. Private property, the value of which is assumed in this commandment, keeps its meaning only as long as this earth lasts. True treasure, as Jesus shows us, can be stored up only in heaven. Jesus himself brought the treasure of heaven to us by coming to establish a lasting kingdom, in which we have an inheritance. That inheritance is his very presence, for he is himself the treasure that we must value above all others.

PROPERTY AND LAND USE IN THE OLD TESTAMENT

But let us first consider the ramifications and implications of this eighth commandment in the context of the Old and New Testaments. Rules about private property and its use take up quite a surprising place in the laws God gave to his people. God cares about physical things. He set up careful structures for ownership, and the children of Israel were to respect the belongings of others. They were not to take a millstone as a pledge, for example, since such an action would deprive a man of his sustenance by keeping him from grinding grain for bread. They were similarly not to take his cloak in promise of repayment of a debt; otherwise, he would have nothing to keep him warm at night.

The land itself was also regulated by careful laws and rules. Although it was principally seen as belonging to the Lord, he laid down careful rules as to how the people were allowed to "own" and use it. As long as they obeyed God and the laws he laid down for use of the land, God promised that the land would produce all that they needed. It was in God's power and of his grace that he provided inheritances in the land he gave them. To Israel he gave, not wilderness, but already cultivated fields, olive orchards, fig trees, vineyards, farmhouses, and towns. These were portioned out to the tribes, and then to extended families and individuals. True, a man too lazy to work would suffer need, but Israelites who plowed and sowed on the inheritance they received from God would not go hungry, and

God made it clear that anyone who would "move [a] boundary stone" was in contempt of his law (Deut. 19:14).

Of course, we see that the Israelites are not faithful to God's commands, and therefore squander the inheritance that God has given them. The land is taken by enemies, and God's people, a treasure in and of themselves, are carried off, with the most precious gold and silver of God's own temple, to Babylon. Even after the disruption of the exile, however, the returning families received their historic inheritances. The year of Jubilee in the law of Moses also provided for redistribution. God's law carefully ensured a fair, built-in "land reform" policy, though we have no record that the Israelites respected it regularly. According to that law, within one generation the impoverished descendants of a family would again have title to the ancestral inheritance.

PROPERTY AND INHERITANCE IN THE NEW TESTAMENT

One would think that these lessons would be sufficient warning to those who had read and understood the Old Testament. Yet the New Testament must reiterate God's command not to steal. Paul warns the Ephesians to stop stealing and to turn to productive labor, which allows Christian generosity: "He who has been stealing must steal no longer, but must work, doing something useful with his own hands, that he may have something to share with those in need" (Eph. 4:28).

The New Testament times were just as fraught with economic immorality as was the Old Testament period. Thieves sometimes dug through mud-brick walls to rob household possessions. Householders might also dig under the dirt floor, or out in the field, to hide their jewels and coins because of such thieves. Money changers, the bankers of those days, offered interest on deposits, but also exacted cruel and exorbitant interest on debts. The cashiers whose tables Jesus overthrew in the court of the temple were men in this profession. Their rates were what the market would bear. Jesus called their operation a den of thieves. But this does not mean that Jesus necessarily condemns all capital gain. In Jesus' parable, the man who wrapped his silver talent in a cloth and buried it was condemned for failing to invest it with a money changer, which was the least he could do to put the money to work. (Roman law put a cap on interest at 12 percent.)

WEALTH UNDER THE ROMANS

Under Roman rule in the Mediterranean world, trade flourished. Craftsmen and merchants prospered in the villages, and trade routes linked the Roman world with Asia, Africa, and even Britain. Wealth was on display in houses of the governing class. The high priests in Jerusalem were millionaires by our standards, with inherited and acquired wealth. Temple taxes brought in a fortune.

We do not often think of Jesus as an economic threat to the Jewish leaders. But his attack on their greed in the temple and the general implications of his radical message threatened their temple income. This challenge may well have influenced their decision to end his life. (Such was also the case for Paul, whose gospel message threatened the livelihood of the silversmiths who profited from the sales of statues of Diana.)

We get a glimpse of the luxurious degeneracy of the rulers of the time when we think of the event that took place in Herod's palace. His tipsy vow after being aroused by the sensual dance of Salome provides a photo op of the spirit of the times. Rather than lose face at a party, Herod would order the beheading of John the Baptist—the one man who told him the truth. What a parable of confused values! Fortunately, although Herod was able to steal John's lifeblood, he could not steal from him his eternal life, or his place at the banquet table of the Giver of Life and of all good things.

Herod's extravagance was typical of much of Roman society at the time. One colonnaded mansion that has been excavated had a long section of baths, ranging from very hot to very cold. There were public baths in Roman colonies, but the wealthy built their own. There was a middle class, and Jewish culture respected manual labor (though not weaving—a woman's work). But the story of Lazarus living on scraps at the gate of Dives shows the total contrast between great wealth and constant hunger.

OUR TRUE INHERITANCE

Jesus comes on the scene of this decadence with a message to address economics and the morality of wealth. But he does not call Israel back to the earthly inheritance in the land of Canaan, even though God had promised the land as his gift to Israel. "He drove out nations before them and allotted their lands to them as an inheritance; he settled the tribes of Israel in their homes" (Ps. 78:55). The individual Psalmist could sing, "LORD, you have assigned me my portion and my cup; you have made my lot secure. The boundary lines have fallen for me in pleasant places; surely I have a delightful inheritance" (Ps. 16:5–6). King David wrote that psalm. And though he certainly loved Bethlehem, he is surely thinking of a better inheritance than a plot of land near Bethlehem. David uses the symbol of real estate to describe the blessing of his inheritance from the Lord—the inheritance of God's promise to him, the promise of God's blessing on him and his line. Surely at the coming of the

King, the kingdom would be restored and the people of God would be given back their true inheritance.

But what is their true inheritance? Were the Jews expecting to gain back their territory? Were the disciples able to see past liberation from the Roman occupation to a greater liberation? The question was evidently up for discussion among the disciples as well as others who heard Jesus' message. Isaiah had made it clear that the earthly inheritance of the people of God was subject to destruction by invaders, to pollution by sin, and to famine by drought. The prophet Isaiah foretells this judgment: "The earth will be completely laid waste and totally plundered . . . The earth dries up and withers . . . The earth is defiled by its people . . . (Isa. 24:3–5). Hosea also draws attention to the land's pollution from the people's sin:

> There is no faithfulness, no love, no acknowledgment of God in the land. There is only cursing, lying and murder, stealing and adultery; they break all bounds, and bloodshed follows bloodshed. Because of this the land mourns, and all who live in it waste away; the beasts of the field and the birds of the air and the fish of the sea are dying. (Hos. 4:1b–3)

But whether the disciples first understood the principle or not, Jesus' death and resurrection made it clear to them and to other Christians that Christ had brought them an inheritance of a different sort. The apostle Peter affirms the opposite of what Isaiah had foretold. He declares that our inheritance is indestructible, undefiled, and unwithering (1 Peter 1:4). Nothing can happen to our inheritance, for it is reserved in heaven for those of us, as Peter then adds, "who through faith are shielded by God's power until the coming of the salvation that is ready to be revealed in the last time" (1 Peter 1:5). Peter understood that our true inheritance is not a physical land, which can be snatched away by invaders. Our inheritance is kept for us, and we are kept alive to receive it. For both these reasons, our blessing, by faith, is secure. It is not the land of Israel, but a much greater Promised Land.[2]

THE PRIESTLY INHERITANCE FOR ALL BELIEVERS

Even the final Promised Land, however, is not our full inheritance. There is more to it than that. From the symbol of the land as blessing, there sounds a deeper note: the inheritance of Levi. In the distribution of the land as an inheritance, the tribe of Levi was left out. To Aaron the priest, God said, "You will have no inheritance in their land, nor will you have any share among them; I am your share and your inheritance among the Israelites" (Num. 18:20).

Not a strip of land, but the Lord himself would be the inheritance of the priestly tribe. Theirs was the charge of caring for the tabernacle, the tent of God among them, and later the temple. They alone could minister in the holy things. The offerings of the people provided for the priests. This income was not their inheritance, however. The Lord was their inheritance, their lot, and their treasure forever.

The privilege of the priests was made the privilege of all the people of God through Christ. Peter writes, "But you are a chosen people, a royal priesthood, a holy nation, a people belonging to God, that you may declare the praises of him who called you out of darkness into his wonderful light" (1 Peter 2:9). Such an understanding was already present in the Old Testament. In Habakkuk 3:17–18 we read, "Though the fig tree does not bud and there are no grapes on the vines, though the olive crop fails and the fields produce no food, though there are no sheep in the pen and no cattle in the stalls, yet I will rejoice in the LORD, I will be joyful in God my Savior." Here already, we see the notion that God is indeed the inheritance of the land.

THE HOLY SPIRIT AS OUR DOWN PAYMENT

Paul expands this notion of our possession of the Lord when he describes the Holy Spirit, who indwells the believer. The Holy Spirit is the down payment on our inheritance. We *possess* the Spirit—the gift of the Spirit is the promise of the Father. At Pentecost Jesus sent the Spirit from heaven that the church might have the power and wisdom of the Spirit to carry the gospel to the nations. A down payment is not a promissory note. It is cash. What is given is the first installment of what is to come. Amazingly, we receive the presence of the Lord in the gift of the Spirit. Our inheritance is more than the blessings of glory, more than the new heavens and earth. It is the Lord, who gives himself to us, that we may be one with him. Yes, Jesus Christ does all this in transforming the commandment of property rights, "You shall not steal." He gives himself as our treasure.

WE ARE GOD'S INHERITANCE

Further, the Lord also claims *us* as *his* inheritance. Jesus himself came to claim his pearl beyond price. He bought us as his with the cost of his blood. In the Old Testament, the Lord chose Israel as his people from all the nations of the earth. He chose them not for their size as a nation, but simply because he loved them. David prayed, "Save your people and bless your inheritance; be their shepherd and carry them forever" (Ps. 28:9).

Isaiah promises that the Lord will claim not only Israel but even enemy nations as his own. He describes a highway from Egypt to Assyria. "The Assyrians will go to Egypt and the Egyptians to Assyria. The Egyptians and Assyrians will worship together" (Isa. 19:23). What an astonishing picture! Worshipers from the enemy nations will pass right through Israel with no stop at the temple in Jerusalem. The blessing of the Lord will be given to the enemy nations as well as to Israel: "The LORD Almighty will bless them, saying, 'Blessed be Egypt my people, Assyria my handiwork, and Israel my inheritance'" (Isa. 19:25). The intimate terms for God's own people are now given to their enemies.

Isaiah's prophecy foresees a transformation that can come only when the Lord comes. Jesus Christ claims the people of God as his people. His Father in heaven gave his people to his Son, those who were chosen in him from all eternity. In his prayer before going to the cross, Jesus could say, "I have revealed you to those whom you gave me out of the world. They were yours; you gave them to me and they have obeyed your word" (John 17:6).

Jesus, the Good Shepherd, knew that he could keep those whom the Father had given him. "My sheep listen to my voice; I know them, and they follow me. I give them eternal life, and they shall never perish; no one can snatch them out of my hand." He added, "No one can snatch them out of my Father's hand. I and the Father are one" (John 10:27–30). No one can steal the inheritance of the divine Shepherd. As we are the inheritance, the property of the Lord, so, too, we possess our inheritance in Christ. We belong to Jesus; he belongs to us.

THE SPIRIT'S GIFTS AS OUR INHERITANCE

Christ gives us his Spirit to provide life and assurance. Through his Spirit, Christ also provides gifts to serve him. In Luke 19, Jesus told a story about a wealthy man who went to a distant country to claim a kingdom. He gave varying sums of money to his servants to use until he returned. We still speak of "talents"—the large monetary figure used in the parable for a weight of silver. When the king returned, the man who had been given ten talents had gained ten more, the servant entrusted with five had five more, but the man with one talent unwrapped his one talent and presented it in mint condition. He hadn't risked using it; he hadn't even risked a money fund with the bankers.

Is Jesus recommending risk on the stock market? Both of the commended investors had doubled their money while their master was away. If our stock markets are uncertain, were the moneylenders in Jesus' day more dependable? Clearly, Jesus is recommending risk. He assumes, it seems, that risk was involved in securing the returns gained by Mr. Ten and Mr. Five. In the parable, Jesus teaches us about stewardship. He is the King of the kingdom. He must die and rise again, then go up to glory to rule. Luke informs us that Jesus told the parable because "the people thought that the kingdom of God was going to appear at once" (Luke 19:11). While Jesus is gone, he provides gifts to carry forward his saving rule. Those who serve him are his managers, investing the abilities he provides to advance his cause. Our use of his gifts is compared to the job of a broker, investing other people's money.

Is there risk? The apostle Paul could recite his sufferings as he used the gifts the Lord had given him. Those gifts were given so that he might proclaim the gospel to the Gentiles, and stand before hostile synagogues and royal courts. After his conversion and his witness to the Jews in Damascus and Jerusalem, he had to escape threats on his life at both places. For years afterward he was in Tarsus (his hometown, in what is now Turkey). There Barnabas came to find him, and from that day on, Paul's talents were fully invested.

Christ's kingdom is not at risk, however. At times we may feel that our attempts to serve the Lord have brought disaster rather than advance in the work of the kingdom. We may not realize what we are doing. Yet no steward of Christ's gifts is ever alone. The Lord is not an absentee king. Take heart! Even your awkward attempts to live the gospel are guided by the Spirit into the accomplishment of God's purposes. By his Word and Spirit, he guides us, using even our mistakes to bring blessing. In our experience we prove out, as Paul says, the will of God. We are not only servants and stewards, but also children. In union with Christ we are sons of God.

THE EXTRAVAGANCE OF LOVE

Our use of God's gifts marks who we are. The opposite of stealing is giving, as Paul pointed out in his advice to thieves. They were not only to stop stealing, but to work hard, earning money that they could give away. As Christians, if we are to obey the commandment not to steal, we must be full of generosity. That means giving money to the poor, giving of our goods and of our time to Christians in need, giving until it hurts. Judas watched Mary pour about a pint of pure spikenard on the feet of Jesus, and wipe his feet with her hair. He was disgusted: "Why wasn't this perfume sold and the money given to the poor? It was worth a year's wages" (John 12:5).

Jesus defended the extravagant worship of Mary. He said, "Let her alone; she has kept this for the day of My burial. For the poor you have with you always, but Me you do not have always" (John 12:7–8 NKJV). This translation follows the Greek faithfully, but misses the second meaning of *keep*. In both

Greek and English, the word may mean "preserve" or "observe." Since Mary has poured the perfume out, she is not preserving it. Rather, she knows what is awaiting Jesus in Jerusalem. She understands that he will die. Her anointing anticipates the spices or perfumes that were part of burial observances.

Only Jesus could justify the extravagance of Mary in her gift and her devotion. Only Jesus could claim such extravagance as compared to the care of the poor. Caring for the poor was always the distinctive evidence of the fear of the Lord. Yet because Jesus so spoke of his person and work, and defended Mary, his words have placed care for the poor at the heart of Christian devotion. The Lord Jesus died, rose, and ascended into heaven. We cannot now fall at his feet, nor can we anoint his feet with perfume. But as Jesus said, we do have the poor with us. His words imply that we may do for the least of his brothers what we would do for him. He receives our devotion to the poor as we care for them in extravagance, pouring out on them what we wish we could pour out for him. We can care for the poor, wash their feet, as Jesus washed the feet of his disciples. Serving the poor, we serve those to whom Jesus pointed us. Hospital ministries, shelters, rescue missions, care for the homeless—in being involved in all these, we can show our devotion to Jesus.

AN EXAMPLE OF EXTRAVAGANT LOVE

An expert in the law once asked Jesus, "What must I do to inherit eternal life?" Jesus asked him, "What is written in the Law? . . . How do you read it?" (Luke 10:25–26). He asked the professional view of a legal scholar. The expert knew the right answer: " 'Love the Lord your God with all your heart and with

all your soul and with all your strength and with all your mind';
and, 'Love your neighbor as yourself' " (Luke 10:27).

The scholar did know the law. Jesus himself had given
that same summary. Jesus told him, "You have answered correctly . . . Do this and you will live" (Luke 10:28). All the
teaching of Jesus showed the depth of the law, and therefore
the impossibility of keeping it. The man knew himself as
well as the law. His next question showed his uneasiness.
"Who is my neighbor?" he asked (Luke 10:29). He obviously
wanted to put some limits on this law. If he had to love others as himself, he had better control the number of eligible
neighbors!

Jesus answered his question with the familiar story of the
Good Samaritan. A traveler on the lonely and dangerous road
from Jerusalem down to Jericho was assaulted, robbed,
stripped, and left lying by the road half dead. A priest and a
Levite, both charged with the care of the people of God, ner-
vously hastened by on the other side of the road. They had, they
remembered, urgent business in Jericho. The caregiver who
came by was a Samaritan. The expert in the law would be sure
that no Samaritan could be classified as a neighbor. Hostility
between Jews and Samaritans in those days was similar to that
between Jews and Palestinians in our day—but even more
deeply religious.

The Samaritan could have done no more for his own brother
than he did for the victim by the road. He tended his wounds from
his own traveling supply of wine and oil, bandaged him, presumably tearing up one of his own garments, and put him on his own
donkey for the journey down to Jericho. There he suspended his
journey to nurse the man. When the man was out of danger, he
paid his motel bill, covering a period for convalescence. If more
funds were needed, he would pay the bill when he returned.

Jesus showed how he transformed the law by this story, and by the question he asked. Jesus said, "Which of these three do you think was a neighbor to the man who fell into the hands of robbers?" (Luke 10:36). Jesus does not suggest that we ask, "Who is my neighbor? How many must I love?" He wants us to ask, "To whom am I a neighbor? To how many can I show unmeasured love?"

The context of the story is the ministry of Jesus, who not only showed unfailing love to his enemies, but made that love the model of our love—toward God and toward our own enemies. Again the transforming model is the love of Jesus. His is the love that fulfills the law. The commandment "You shall not kill" becomes "Remember my love, take up your cross, and follow me." "And if someone wants to sue you and take your tunic, let him have your cloak as well" (Matt. 5:40).

THE RIGHTS OF DISCIPLES

Our culture demands rights. Crowds riot to demand rights, sometimes even the rights of others, that do need to be respected. Yet Jesus gave the greatest right, the right to be called children of God. That right does not square with the desire of James and John to be first in the kingdom. Peter learned the bitter price of pride when he denied his Lord three times. After the Spirit of Christ had humbled Peter, he understood how the love of Jesus called for total devotion and utter humility. Peter charged leaders in the church of Christ, "Clothe yourselves with humility toward one another, because, 'God opposes the proud but gives grace to the humble.' Humble yourselves, therefore, under God's mighty hand, that he may lift you up in due time" (1 Peter 5:5b–6).

In the power of Christ and his love we can learn not only to refrain from stealing what belongs to others, but to multiply our treasure by clinging to Christ alone. Out of the bounty of that miraculous multiplication of our gifts and treasure, we can amply supply those whom Christ places in our path. Let us shower on those around us the treasure God has given us, not counting the cost, but looking to that treasure that is laid up in heaven for us, namely, Christ himself.

STUDY QUESTIONS

Think It Through:

1. What actions of the wealthy and powerful could be considered a form of stealing from widows and orphans?

2. What remedy for stealing did Paul present to a thief? (Eph. 4:28)

3. Why were the priests and Sadducees so enraged by Jesus' cleansing of the temple? How did Jesus characterize the market and banking conducted in the court of the temple? (Jer. 7:11; Mark 11:17)

4. How did Jesus transform the commandment, "You shall not steal"?

5. Peter says that our inheritance cannot be destroyed or defiled and that it cannot wither (1 Peter 1:4). Look at Isaiah 24:3–5, however, where the prophet predicts that exactly these things will happen to Israel's earthly inheritance. Yet our inheritance is kept for us, and we are kept for our inheritance. How does the Lord keep us? (1 Peter 1:6–7)

6. How is the Lord our inheritance? How are we his?

7. How do we invest for the Lord? (Matt. 25:14–30) From this parable we get our use of the word *talents*. Why is the Lord's warning so severe for the servant who did not invest?

Take It to Heart:

1. The Old Testament law had a double tithe. In the New Testament, Jesus asks us to give all to him and to be his steward of our money, time, and abilities. Consider how you can give all your life to him. No partitions remain. It is all his. Do you sense joy as you bring everything to him? That joy expresses freedom from bondage to the secrets we would keep from him.

2. How can your spiritual gifts be invested where you are now? Have you been tempted to think that you have no gifts with which to serve? Ask the Lord to help you see the need, and begin to help. You will discover your gifts, not by taking inventory, but by serving.

3. Worship must always be extravagant. Reflect on John 12:1–8. How did Mary's worship of Jesus show extravagance?

10

THE NINTH COMMANDMENT

The Lord, the Truth

"You shall not give false testimony against your neighbor."
(Ex. 20:16)

The commandment "You shall not give false testimony against your neighbor" implies a court situation. Someone is being accused before a judge of words or actions that the person has not said or committed. Such court trials are not unique to our society. Nearly every culture in the world has some kind of tribunal to adjudicate disagreements between individuals.

FALSE WITNESSES IN THE BIBLE

The Old Testament is full of examples of false witnesses. For example, Queen Jezebel hired false witnesses to get something for her husband, King Ahab. Ahab was pouting because Naboth would not sell him the family vineyard. Jezebel said, "Is this how you act as king over Israel? Get up and eat! Cheer up.

I'll get you the vineyard of Naboth . . ." (1 Kings 21:7). She paid false witnesses to testify that Naboth had cursed God and the king. They then stoned Naboth, and Ahab took the vineyard. When he went to survey it, there stood the prophet Elijah, with a word from the Lord for Ahab! No one else was able to stand up for Naboth, but the Lord saw. The Lord heard those words, uttered in contempt of his command.

The false witnesses against Naboth had no words to twist. They manufactured a complete lie. More often, false witnesses gain credibility by using some aspect of the truth to support their lies. Satan, the Liar and Father of Lies, is a master at dissembling. He usually edits what God has said, as he did with Adam and Eve. God had told them that they were not to eat of the tree of knowledge of good and evil. Satan's version was: "Did God really say, 'You must not eat from *any* tree in the garden?'" (Gen. 3:1). Apparently, the twist he gave to God's words was enough to sow the seeds of doubt in Eve's mind.

Another innocent man once stood before a judge, faced with false witnesses, hired to testify against the one person in all of history who never spoke anything untrue. The Sanhedrin had difficulty getting two witnesses to agree in false testimony about Jesus. At last they found two who would distort what Jesus had said about the temple. They pretended that Jesus had threatened to destroy it.

Christ's followers have stood many times before the bench to hear flagrant lies about them told to the court. In this, we are promised as Christians, we will share in Christ's sufferings. False witnesses lied about Stephen, the first witness to Christ who sealed his testimony with his blood. (*Martyr* is the word for "witness.") Again, the false witnesses put a different spin on what Stephen had said. "This fellow," they said, "never stops speaking against the holy place and against the law. For we have heard him say that this Jesus of Nazareth will destroy this place and change the customs Moses handed down to us" (Acts 6:13–14). That charge recycled the false charge against Jesus, that he threatened to destroy the temple. It also reflected a core of truth. Stephen had probably spoken of how Jesus had fulfilled the law and had given his body, the true temple, on the cross. As we can see from these examples, and as we know from the fabric of our own lives and experiences, there are many ways of misrepresenting the truth. Christians throughout the ages have been falsely charged by someone twisting their words.

If you have never seen the movie *A Man for All Seasons*, you must get a copy. Thomas More, realizing the danger of false witnesses, decided that his only course in resisting Henry VIII, whose marriage Thomas did not approve, was to remain silent. He decided never to utter any opinion about the marriage, whether in public or in private. There is a very moving scene in this film, in which his simple and faithful wife feels hurt because Thomas won't trust her and tell her what he really thinks about the marriage of the king. Thomas gently takes her hand and gets her to play out an imaginary scene: "Now we are before the judge," he says to his wife. "You have sworn on God's Word that you will tell the truth. I am the judge and I ask you, 'Has your husband ever told you what he thinks of the king's marriage?' What will you say?" His wife then realizes that Thomas is really trying to protect her by refusing to speak his mind. In the end, Thomas's tongue is loosed because there is no longer any point in keeping silent. A young acquaintance becomes a false witness and claims to have heard Thomas's opinions.

Our courts attempt to screen out the variety of lies by insisting that we tell "the truth, the whole truth, and nothing but the truth." In this realm, however, the courts depend on a biblical understanding of one's word. They must assume that there is such a thing as truth, and that a person who stands in court is willing to speak the truth. As in the movie just mentioned, the courts used to ask us to swear by our Christian conscience (by placing our hand on the sacred Word of God) that we would speak the truth. But the admonition to "speak the whole truth" is insufficient for those willing to make words mean what they want them to. We can hardly help but think of our own former president, perjuring himself before the courts of our land by pretending that one could put several interpretations on the word *is*.

THE COURTROOM

The courtroom setting often appears in the Bible. For example, when the people of Israel complained in the desert that they were going to die of thirst, they brought their complaint as a charge against God. They demanded a hearing. The name "Meribah," given to the incident, includes the root *rib*, which means "a legal process." They were ready to stone Moses as the execution of judicial sentence. They would not die of thirst until they had court-martialed Moses and found him guilty of treason. He had led them into a waterless desert. The term *Marah* in this context also means "trial," as in a court of law. Since their charge was really against God, not Moses, the Lord ordered a hearing, with the elders of the people as witnesses. Then God, the Rock of Israel, stood on the Rock before Moses, and received the blow of punishment as though he had been guilty.

At a later time, Samuel wanted to report on his life as a judge and prophet of the people of God. He presented his defense as though he had been charged with oppression, graft, and stealing. He called upon the Lord to be his witness, as well as the king and the people. The witness of the people secured his acquittal: "Not guilty!" (1 Sam. 12:1–5). Samuel then used the format of a trial to put God on the stand, and to secure vindication for him.

Says Samuel to the people: "Now then, stand still and see this great thing the LORD is about to do before your eyes! Is it not wheat harvest now? I will call upon the LORD to send thunder and rain. And you will realize what an evil thing you did in the eyes of the LORD when you asked for a king" (1 Sam. 12:16–17). God himself provided the verdict when he sent a rainstorm in the month of May—testimony to the truth and faithfulness of the Lord (see the entire story in 1 Samuel 12:6–18).

Other legal cases include Job, David, and Isaiah. The book of Job uses the format of a law case, in which Job's friends are prosecuting a case against him. They seek a confession of guilt. Job appeals to God as his witness: "Even now my witness is in heaven; my advocate is on high" (Job 16:19). David describes charges filed against him, and calls upon God to defend his cause: "Vindicate me, O God, and plead my cause against an ungodly nation" (Ps. 43:1). "Contend, O LORD, with those who contend with me; fight against those who fight against me" (Ps. 35:1). David's enemies not only bring charges, but also threaten armed assaults. "Ruthless witnesses come forward; they question me on things I know nothing about" (Ps. 35:11). Witnesses in the ancient Near East would prosecute as well as giving testimony. Isaiah pictures the Lord himself presenting the charges against Israel: "The LORD stands up to plead, and stands to judge the people" (Isa. 3:13 NKJV). He charges the elders and princes with grinding the faces of the poor, while their women walk with jingling jewelry and nose jewels (Isa. 3:14–23). The Lord bears witness against them, and proceeds to judgment.

WITNESS AND EVIDENCE

Witness differs from evidence. Witness involves people, whereas evidence is "neutral" fact. The skid marks of a car may be measured as evidence, but they must be seen in context. Doubt is appropriate. Were the skid marks made by the car involved in the accident? Does the length of the mark indicate how fast the car was going? Witness is different, for a person is giving testimony to what was seen or heard. To doubt a witness is to disbelieve what he says.

But when we believe or disbelieve God, who acts as witness? How can we put God on trial, as the children of Israel were ready to do in the desert? God appears as his own witness in the covenant he made with Israel at Sinai. He testifies to his redemption of Israel as his own people. The covenant he made with them was sealed as his testimony in the tablets of stone. The ninth commandment against false witness is inscribed on the tablet as part of God's testimony to his people. It was itself a witness, by its very existence, to the reality of the covenant made by the Lord with Israel at Mount Sinai. To keep the precious tablets safe, they were put inside the Ark of the Testimony.

The Magna Carta of England and the Declaration of Independence of the United States are historical documents of the first order. They are more than mementos from the past, for they still carry legal authority. Yet the law God gave to Israel was a unique testimony to the covenant that God made with Israel. The psalm given to Moses and those of the later psalmists of Israel were not simply Israel's response to God's revelation. They were also, like the Ten Commandments, the Lord's witness against them in their rebellion and disobedience (Deut. 31:19).

In the Old Testament, two or three witnesses were necessary before a man could be condemned of a crime. But to vindicate God, what witnesses can we find? God himself and his Word are seen in Hebrews as the two witnesses necessary. Hebrews 6:16 and following speaks of a conundrum—God swearing to be faithful to his covenant. The author says that men always swear by something greater than themselves. By what can God swear, then? God himself is the first witness, and his Word is the second witness, authenticating his promise.

Jesus is also called a witness: the "faithful witness, the firstborn from the dead, and the ruler of the kings of the earth" (Rev. 1:5). God bears witness to himself, then, by the witness of the Son to the Father, of the Spirit to the Son, and of the Father to the Son. The Father in heaven is a witness to Christ, in that the Scriptures witness to him: "These are the Scriptures that testify about me, yet you refuse to come to me to have life" (John 5:39b–40). The witness of Jesus to his own mission from the Father is verified by his miracles, which are also witnessing signs to the truth of his claims. This may seem somewhat cyclical, but God must swear only by himself, for there is no one and nothing that stands above him. How gracious, then, of God to allow us to serve as witnesses to his promises.

God allows *us* to serve as his witnesses. The Bible is full of situations in which God's people are witnesses to his faithfulness in keeping his promises. Throughout the Old Testament, God's people bore witness to God's name among the nations. Individuals bore witness as they stood up under persecution and suffering, or as they attempted to reestablish faithfulness to the Word of God in Israel. The prophets bore witness to God as they proclaimed his Word, at the cost of their comfort and even their lives. In the New Testament, John the Baptist serves as the first witness to the person of Jesus Christ, the Light of the World.

APOSTOLIC WITNESS

The role of the apostles as witnesses is unique. Although we as Christian brothers and sisters are called upon to serve as witnesses to the gospel and to the work of Jesus Christ, the apostles played a special role. They were with him and served as eyewitnesses to his deeds and earwitnesses to his teaching. Jesus declared, "And this gospel of the kingdom will be preached in the whole world as a testimony to all nations, and then the end will come" (Matt. 24:14).

When the church chose another apostle to replace Judas, they looked for one who had been with Jesus from the beginning. The author of the book of Hebrews reminds us that the salvation announced by the Lord "was confirmed to us by those who heard him. God also testified to it by signs, wonders and various miracles, and gifts of the Holy Spirit distributed according to his will" (Heb. 2:3b–4).

Peter described the calling of the apostles after the resurrection this way: "We are witnesses of these things, and so is the Holy Spirit, whom God has given to those who obey him" (Acts 5:32). The apostles wrote down and preached what they had heard from Jesus. But we no longer have living eyewitnesses of Jesus' doings. Their written witness now stands in the place of that spoken witness, and it is the witness of the Spirit that now assures our hearts that Christ's work is indeed what the apostles said it was. The Lord continues to bear witness to the truth of Christ's work as he works in our hearts through the Holy Spirit, who uses the Scripture to assure us of Christ's finished work. The intercession of the Spirit for us is joined with the assurance of the Spirit that we have been made children of God (Rom. 8:16). The Spirit himself testifies with our spirit that we are God's children. The Spirit pours out in our hearts the love of God for us. The knowledge that the Lord loves us is his witness in our hearts.

OBJECTS AS WITNESSES

The Bible is full of "witnesses" to the power of God. We have seen that witness requires personal testimony. But we also see that the "evidence," which we have called "neutral" in the case of the traffic accident, is in fact not really neutral. Because God is the one who created the world by the power of his Spirit, we find that everything in the world is really a testimony to his power and presence. In the Bible, we find hundreds of objects and customs that have been made witnesses. The tabernacle is known as the "tent of the testimony" (Num. 17:7). Why? Because it housed the ark of the covenant in which the tablets inscribed by God were kept. Why are tablets considered a testimony? Because the tablets of the law were written by God, and given to Moses as a personal message to the people. It is as if God's signature were to be clearly recognized on them. So we see that the Ten Commandments themselves, God's words in God's writing, are a testimony, a witness to the living God.

In modern Jerusalem is a crypt commemorating the Holocaust, when six million Jews were gassed, then burned in the ovens of Hitler's camps. The memorial is called *Yad vashem*, "a hand and a name." *Hand* is a term for a marker. Saul set up a "hand" after his victory over the Amalekites (1 Sam. 15:15). This marker, like other objects, was a memorial or a witness. Jacob set up the stone pillow on which he had slept at Bethel as a witness to the promise God made to him in the dream he had that night of the stairway from heaven. The Lord had descended to be with Jacob and to repeat the promise he had made to Abraham. Jacob anointed the stone as "Bethel," "the house of God." "God was in this place, and I didn't know it," Jacob said.

Later, when Jacob made a covenant with his uncle Laban, Laban set up a pile of stones and a pillar as a witness to the covenant. Laban said:

> Here is this heap, and here is this pillar I have set up between you and me. This heap is a witness, and this pillar is a witness, that I will not go past this heap to your side to harm you

and that you will not go past this heap and pillar to my side to harm me. May the God of Abraham and the God of Nahor, the God of their father, judge between us. (Gen. 31:51–53a)

This oath by Laban was matched by an oath taken by Jacob in the name of the Fear of his father, Isaac. They called upon God to judge their controversy. Jacob then offered sacrifice. They ate the sacrificial meal together and spent the night there. The pillar and stones are set up not merely as boundary stones, but also as testimonies to their covenant.

THE NEW COVENANT: THE SPIRIT AS WITNESS

In the New Covenant, we do not see believers setting up stones or objects as witnesses or testimonies anymore. Though Paul and Barnabas shook off the dust of Antioch against the unbelief of the synagogue in that city, we have no record of objects made to be witnesses. Paul used the altar to an unknown God as a witness to the ignorance of paganism, but he did not describe it as a covenant witness. The reason God's people no longer need such objects is that the apostles themselves brought the Lord's witness in the power of the Holy Spirit. The concrete signs of God's faithfulness to his promises are the sacraments he instigated. We now have baptism and the Lord's Supper as memorials to God's faithfulness to his covenant.

In this, too, we see the transforming work of Christ. The tabernacle of testimony is not replicated in a cathedral, but it is seen in the bread of the Lord's Supper and the cup of the New Covenant in Christ's blood. The mystery of Christ's presence in Communion shows his transforming of the witness symbols of the Old Testament. The elements are indeed witnesses to his atoning death and risen life. They are not mere memorials, however, for Christ is spiritually present. In the Eucharist, the Lord

Jesus brings again the assurance of his love. The Holy Spirit bears witness with our spirits, as we sit together at the Lord's Table.

So what becomes of witness in the New Covenant? Is there no place for witness and testimony? If we cannot set up piles of stones or go to a temple with symbols of God's presence, how are we to show witness to the gospel in this post-resurrection period? True witness in the New Covenant is witness before the nations. "You are my witnesses," the Lord said to his chosen people in the Old Testament. The risen Lord Jesus instructed his disciples to wait in Jerusalem until they received the Spirit and the promised gift of the Father. "You will receive power when the Holy Spirit comes on you; and you will be my witnesses in Jerusalem, and in all Judea and Samaria, and to the ends of the earth" (Acts 1:8).

Luke uses these words of Christ as the outline for the book of Acts. Witness to the gospel spreads from Jerusalem to Rome. The cosmic law case, in which God is "in the dock,"[1] so to speak, is still being played out in our time. In Isaiah chapters 40–55, God calls the nations to hear: "Be silent before me, you islands! Let the nations renew their strength! Let them come forward and speak; let us meet together at the place of judgment" (Isa. 41:1).

God's law case as described in the prophets is finally coming to trial, now that Christ has come. But in some sense, the law itself is changed as Christ stands in the dock. All justice is summed up and transformed in the person of Christ. He transforms it by his victory on the cross, his resurrection, and his ascension, and through his gift of the Spirit. Christ's Spirit comes as the promised Advocate who convicts the world of sin, righteousness, and judgment. The Spirit also vindicates the righteousness of God, and overturns the conviction of Christ by his enemies. The Jewish Sanhedrin found Jesus guilty of blasphemy and condemned him to death. Pilate, the Roman procurator, sentenced him to be crucified for claiming to be the king of the Jews. The Spirit, however, through the testimony of the apostles, witnesses to Christ as the Righteous One. The apostles testify to the injustice of the crucifixion. Jesus promised to send the Spirit of truth:

> When he comes, he will convict the world of guilt in regard to sin and righteousness and judgment: in regard to sin, because men do not believe in me; in regard to righteousness, because I am going to the Father, where you can see me no longer; and in regard to judgment, because the prince of this world now stands condemned. (John 16:8–11)

The Spirit convicts. As the Spirit of truth, he reveals the righteousness of God, and exposes sin. The conviction of the Spirit will be revealed at the day of judgment. Yet the convicting power of the Spirit appears in mercy when the sinner confesses his sin and flees to Christ to receive the gift of his righteousness. "If we confess our sins, he is faithful and just and will forgive us our sins and purify us from all unrighteousness" (1 John 1:9). The Spirit reveals the righteousness of God in his justifying verdict for sinners. On the other hand, the Spirit also reveals the righteousness of God in condemning the impenitent, who scorn the incredible grace of God in the gift of his Son. In the Spirit, Jesus calls the nations to come to him in repentance. Jesus was filled with the Spirit in his ministry on earth, and he, with the Father, gives the Spirit for the task of witness.

In the witness of the Spirit, we see the very opposite of the sin mentioned in the ninth commandment. The Spirit does not bear false witness against anyone. All his witness is entirely and utterly pure and true. That witness cuts into our souls and consciences, dividing bone from marrow. It causes the truth to be a savor of life to life and of death to death (2 Cor. 2:16). And that witness is available to us as believers because the Spirit who moves in our hearts has committed the truth of Christ's life, death, and resurrection to an infallible witness, that of the Scriptures.

THE SCRIPTURES AS WITNESS

Our witness is the Scriptures because the witness of Scripture is to the Lord. We have no more use for an ark or the stone tablets it held. That testimony has been fulfilled in the writings of the apostles and prophets in the New Testament. Peter summarizes the apostolic witness when he speaks to the Gentile centurion Cornelius. In preaching the gospel to Cornelius and the other Gentiles with him in his house that day, Peter described the witness of the apostles to everything that Jesus did, and to his crucifixion and resurrection. The apostles ate and drank with Jesus after he rose from the dead. "He commanded us to preach to the people and to testify that he is the one whom God appointed as judge of the living and the dead. All the prophets testify about him that everyone who believes in him receives forgiveness of sins through his name" (Acts 10:42–43). This same apostolic witness was recorded in the Scriptures of the New Testament for our benefit. We can have the same confidence that Cornelius and his friends and family had in hearing the testimony and witness of the apostles.

PERSONAL TESTIMONY AS WITNESS

But we often define *witness* as our own "testimony" of God's grace in our lives. We recount how God has been gracious in saving us. In our day and culture in a postmodern world, however, such witness bears little weight. "So you have had a religious experience? Great! I'm glad for you! I've had a few, too." When we bear witness to Christ's name, we must not be content to speak of personal experience, though this is, of course, not to be excluded. We must join our own witness to that of the apostles and prophets, and even to the witness of Jesus to the Old Testament. Without such roots, our own experience remains what our non-Christian friends have said: "a religious experience." Our witness will have power only insofar as the Spirit is its power, and the power of the Spirit is his testimony to the Word of Christ. The words of Scripture must be stored in our minds so that we can appeal to them in the context of our witness to others. We don't simply quote Scripture at people, but the Scripture lends authority to our witness, and we do well to have it on the tip of our tongues. As we witness to Christ's truth and love and to the sacrifice he made for us on the cross, we must trust the Spirit's gifts to us. The Spirit gives us words to speak—not on the level of the inspiration of Scripture, of course. He illumines our minds to understand not only what the Word says, but what the person says to whom we speak, or the response of groups that we address. Jesus told us to trust him for words when we stand on trial for our faith: "When they arrest you, do not worry about what to say or how to say it. At that time you will be given what to say, for it will not be you speaking, but the Spirit of your Father speaking through you" (Matt. 10:19–20). In our witness we do affirm God's witness as our own. We challenge the patterns of unbelief, and affirm the realities of faith. We believe; therefore, we speak.

CORPORATE WITNESS

Witness is not just an individual affair, even if the Spirit does testify to our individual hearts that we are children of God. The church as a whole is also a witness, a community of witnesses. When the Lord gave the Spirit on Pentecost, the disciples bore witness to the reality of the resurrection of Jesus, and of his saving death. Peter writes, "You are a chosen people, a royal priesthood, a holy nation, a people belonging to God, that you may declare the praises of him who called you out of darkness into his wonderful light" (1 Peter 2:9). There is a sense in which the gathered witness of the church is crucial in our witness to Christ. In speaking to the Corinthian church, Paul explains to them how important the details of their worship are for the sake of witness. A worship service in which the gathered people of God are speaking out the witness of the Scriptures will produce in the unbeliever who comes in the wonderful response, "God is really among you!" (1 Cor. 14:24–25). The blood of the saints is mingled as it cries out in testimony to the truth of the gospel. That corporate witness spans the globe and spans the eons of history. Christ's church bears witness from the time of Adam and will continue to do so until Christ returns in judgment and glory.

In its witness, the church does not draw attention to itself, but to Jesus. Satan, the Liar and Deceiver, bears false witness against the Word and work of God. But Jesus is the Truth. His word alone, his unsupported witness, has enough weight to guarantee its veracity: "Even if I testify on my own behalf, my testimony is valid, for I know where I came from and where I am going" (John 8:14). Yet Jesus always has another Witness, the witness of his Father. "I stand with the Father, who sent me. In your own Law it is written that the testimony of two men is valid. I am one who testifies for myself; my other witness is the Father who sent me" (John 8:16b–18). John the Baptist was a shining lamp in witnessing to Jesus, but no mere man could provide the witness of the Father, who spoke from heaven: "This is my Son, whom I love; with him I am well pleased" (Matt. 3:17).

OLD TESTAMENT WITNESS TO JESUS

The Old Testament bore witness to Jesus. He told his enemies, "If you believed Moses, you would believe me, for he wrote about me" (John 5:46). Moses is therefore the accuser of the Jewish leaders who refused the testimony of Jesus. "These are the Scriptures that testify about me, yet you refuse to come to me to have life" (John 5:39b–40). Both the *works* of Jesus and the *words* of Jesus are given by the Father. The presence of Jesus is the presence of the Son of God, sent from the Father. After his resurrection, Jesus joined two disciples walking from Jerusalem to Emmaus. Beginning with the books of Moses he went through the prophets of the Old Testament to explain how all the Scriptures were about him.

True witness to the Father is therefore witness to Jesus. He is the Truth incarnate, both in the sense of bringing the reality that fulfills the shadows of the Old Testament and in the sense of revealing the personal reality of God himself, in the person of his Son. True witness to God must be witness to Jesus. Again we see that Jesus fulfilled the Old Testament, not only by coming as the Old Testament promised, but also by bringing the reality to which the Old Testament pointed.

THE FINAL JUDGE

False witness and true witness demand a verdict from the Judge. Ultimately, false witness and true witness will be sorted out. We will have no questions at the last day as to how particular evidence should be interpreted. Those who reject the true witness of Christ and of his believers are rejecting the one who stands behind those words of testimony—Jesus, and the Father himself. The absolute truthfulness of Jesus' Word will be made clear to all those who have refused to believe it. One day, their false testimony about Christ will be denounced before the throne of the Just Judge of the universe. And at that time, all of Christ's saints who have been persecuted, disbelieved, mocked, and put to the sword will be vindicated in their belief in the veracity of Christ's promises to them. Jesus will bear true witness before the Father on their behalf.

As Jesus transformed the ninth commandment, he shows how we keep it, in life and word, to the praise of his Father. He calls us to a witness of doxological evangelism. Again we see that the commandment is love that leads to praise. The power of the Spirit guides and drives us, providing boldness in witness, making us unashamed of our Savior. This calling goes far beyond a command not to lie about a brother in a court of law. It is a promise to us that Christ himself will defend us before the final court of law. His testimony on our behalf will allow us to enter the throne room of the King without being put to death. The freedom and life that Christ has purchased for us is to be used in joyful testimony and witness of him. To remain silent in a situation that gives us an opportunity to bear witness to our Savior is to deny him before men. We are to witness to the truth of God's witness to Christ and through Christ. It is our high privilege to bear witness in the Spirit.

Yet as John Frame points out in his lectures,[2] witnessing is not so much what we *do* as what we *are*. As believers in Christ, we are *made* witnesses—as Francis Schaeffer used to say, "before the watching world."[3] The stone set up between Jacob and Laban was a witness by its very existence. So are we. Simon Peter, out in the courtyard when Christ was on trial, was a witness. He was recognized as a disciple of Christ. In fear he swore three times that he had never known Jesus. Jesus looked at Peter as the cock crowed, and Peter fled weeping into the night. Yet Jesus had prayed for Peter before his disciple denied him.

Jesus didn't abandon Peter in the midst of his denial, but looked at him, showing that he was personally concerned.

What joy to know that God himself has promised to use us as witnesses. We will often be tempted, as was Peter, to fear man and fail to bring witness to our God. Yet Jesus took that failure, too, to the cross, where it was nailed along with the one who became sin for us. Jesus took on himself all the injustice due to false witnesses. He, above all, suffered for the slander to his name, for the lies that were told of him. And he took the judgment of the Just One, going to the grave for our faithlessness. For that reason, we have confidence that our witness to him will be received by the Father. What joy comes as we speak the name of Jesus! The resurrected Jesus restored Peter, asking him three times, "Simon, son of John, do you love me?" (John 21:15–17). He asks us that question now, having restored us. What can we now do in witness to him, to reach his lost people and to bear witness to his name?

STUDY QUESTIONS

Think It Through:

1. In a court case, how does witness differ from evidence? Why are two witnesses required in Old Testament law? Does this connect with Jesus' reason for sending out the disciples two by two?

2. Why are the Ten Commandments called *witnesses* ("testimonies")?

3. The priests in the Sanhedrin, the Jewish court, had determined to demand the death penalty for Jesus. Yet they could not get two witnesses to agree on what Jesus had said. On what ground did the Sanhedrin convict him? (Mark 14:63–64)

4. How did the priests bear false witness to Pilate about Jesus? Note the "spin" that the enemies of the gospel put on the preaching of Stephen (Acts 6:13–14). How did Paul's enemies in Jerusalem bear false witness against him? (Acts 24:5–6)

5. To what witnesses did Jesus appeal? (John 5:31–37; 8:13–18) Jesus' signs also witnessed to his claims (John 20:30). Why were eye- and earwitnesses necessary in the founding of Christ's church? (Heb. 2:3b–4)

6. We often speak of personal testimonies. That means that we bear witness to the truth of the gospel, and claim that we know this to be true in our own lives and experience. Consider the danger, however, of giving our own testimony without presenting the testimony of the Scriptures. Our postmodern world assumes that everybody has religious experiences. They may differ, but each is true for the person experiencing it. The Word of God is still the sword of the Spirit, the truth of the Lord who speaks.

Take It to Heart:

1. Rejoice in the reality of the testimony of the Holy Spirit in our hearts. The Spirit bears witness with our spirits that we are the children of God. The Spirit pours out the Lord's love in your heart, and assures you that you belong to him. Spend some moments in prayer, thanking him for his presence!

2. Seek the Lord's grace in practicing doxological evangelism. The commandment is love that leads to praise. When your heart is singing, you are ready to tell others about him. Of course, we must speak of him when our hearts are not singing as well! Sometimes the very act of speaking the truth also sets our hearts to singing.

3. Consider how you might twist a person's words or actions to make them appear less than honest, or to cause someone to think badly of them. How can we bear a good witness about our family members, our friends, our neighbors, and our enemies? Think of practical ways of building up the reputation of those you know. How might this benefit the kingdom of Christ?

11

THE TENTH COMMANDMENT

Seeking the King and His Kingdom

"You shall not covet your neighbor's house. You shall not covet your neighbor's wife, or his manservant or maidservant, his ox or donkey, or anything that belongs to your neighbor." (Ex. 20:17)

This last commandment may seem slightly odd to you. The commandments begin with worshiping God, and end with an admonition not to be looking too hard at the sleek donkey next door! It would seem more fitting in this last commandment to have the kind of summary that Jesus gave. And indeed, we can be helped in understanding this command about coveting when we consider Christ's summary.

BEHIND OUR LOVE FOR GOD

Jesus showed us that the Ten Commandments lead to him. They command us to love God, and to love our neighbor. In order to show us how to go about loving our neighbor, Jesus had to take us behind (or above) the love we should show to God, in order to show us that God first loved us. "This is love," John says, "not that we loved God, but that he loved us and sent his Son as an atoning sacrifice for our sins" (1 John 4:10). Jesus, the Son of God, knew the Father's love, and in his love for the Father, he was willing to be separated from the Father on the cross to pay the price of our sin. When we love the one who first loved us, we reflect the saving love of Calvary.

As Jesus explained the Ten Commandments, he showed us how they pointed forward to him. In this way, he shows us how the commandments dig deep into our hearts in demanding obedience. His transformation of them shows us that no formal deeds can ever meet God's real desires for our behavior and attitudes. As we have considered the relation of Jesus to the commandments, we have seen how Jesus constantly points us to the desire of our hearts in following him.

Yet the tenth commandment, a command not to covet, was clearly a "heart" commandment even in the Old Testament. This command does not simply warn the Israelites against stealing the belongings of others. It goes much deeper, requiring that God's people should not even desire what belongs to another. It focuses not on actions but on attitudes. It speaks not just of what we do, but of what we want to do. Of all the neighbor-related commandments, it is the only one that can't be seen by neighbors! Your neighbor need never know that you covet his new BMW. Only God will see that this commandment has been broken, unless, of course, it leads us to break one of the others because our hearts are full of covetousness.

A HEART COMMANDMENT ABOUT DESIRE

Professor John Frame, in his lectures on the Westminster Shorter Catechism, pointed out that this commandment does not condemn desiring. Contrary to Buddhism, the teaching of Jesus does not find liberty in the death of desire. Nor does it encourage a Mennonite rejection of the conveniences brought by industrial, and now electronic, progress. The lines before you, if you have persevered this far, are lines composed on a computer. The tenth commandment does not forbid us to desire the blessings of God's creation or the fruit of human labor. It condemns desiring what belongs to others—envy, in short.[1] Stealing was forbidden in the eighth commandment. In this command, the *desire* to steal is also forbidden. Sin starts in our hearts before it slips merchandise into our pockets, with or without a credit card. Contemporary advertising works very hard to heighten our desires for a sleek sports car or that perfectly divine dress. It taps the natural desires God has given us and attempts to twist them and to play upon them to create envy in our souls. The envy that this commandment forbids is not only a desire for something that belongs to someone else. It is our desire for anything that would draw us away from contentedly serving God wherever in his good providence he has placed us.

When we consider how Jesus has transformed this command, we realize that Jesus is asking of us not less desire, but infinitely more! Jesus commands us to seek the kingdom of God and his righteousness with all our heart. He taught us to pray, "Thy kingdom come. Thy will be done in earth, as it is in heaven" (Matt. 6:10 KJV). Our fixed desire is for the saving power of God's kingdom to be manifested in this world. We seek it now in the work of the Spirit, and in the future in the return of Jesus Christ. We are to covet Christ's mighty work among the nations, and the glory of his coming again in resurrection power and judgment. Jesus himself shows us the passion of such service, as the "zeal" of God's house "consumes" his heart (John 2:17).

It is not wrong to desire the good things of God's creation. We already dealt with some of the implications of a desire for *things* when we discussed stealing and the notion of treasure. Paul has told us that all created things are good. As Christians, we may desire the pleasure that these good things give us, though we are particularly encouraged to desire them not so much for ourselves as for the poor, and for the starving victims of tyrants. Yet we are to desire the blessings of heaven above the choicest of earth's treasures. Our transformed desire turns its longing eyes on the treasure of heaven.

Jesus reminded us of the wealthy man who decided one night to build bigger barns to hold his grain. His only plans for his future were centered on his holdings. He hadn't planned that his soul would be required of him that night. "Store up for yourselves treasures in heaven," Jesus said, "where moth and rust do not destroy, and where thieves do not break in and steal. For where your treasure is, there your heart will be also" (Matt. 6:20–21). I am only a very minor "investor," but I have recently learned, along with many of the "mighty" investors, that earthly treasure in equities is far more risky than coins buried under the earthen floor in biblical times! Jesus asks, "Where is your treasure?" Paul writes, "Since, then, you have been raised with Christ, set your hearts on things above, where Christ is seated at the right hand of God. Set your minds on things above, not on earthly things" (Col. 3:1–2).

This is the treasure that the Rev. Jack Arnold stored up. After retiring from the ministry, he and his wife wore themselves out in selfless service for the kingdom, traveling to scores of small villages and hamlets to encourage Christians in their marriages and to teach them the Word of God. The treasure they stored up for themselves in retirement was kingdom treasure, not stocks and bonds. When Jack died on January 11, 2005, the Drudge Report picked up on the story:

The Rev. Jack Arnold, 69, was nearing the end of his sermon Sunday at Covenant Presbyterian Church in this Orlando suburb when he grabbed the podium before falling to the floor, said the Rev. Michael S. Beates, associate pastor at Covenant Presbyterian. Before collapsing, Arnold quoted the 18th century Bible scholar, John Wesley, who said, "Until my work on this earth is done, I am immortal. But when my work for Christ is done . . . I go to be with Jesus."[2]

For Jack, as for all Christ's disciples, the treasure of heaven is Christ himself, the Lord of heaven. We do not set our minds on rewards that may be ours, but on Jesus. We desire the Lord more than his gifts. Paul regarded everything as rubbish in order to "gain Christ and be found in him . . ." (Phil 3:8b–9a). The one who delights in the Lord finds in him the desire of his heart.

SEEK FIRST THE KINGDOM

Jesus gave his disciples a prayer to direct the desire of their hearts. He instructed us to pray that God would be glorified—that his name would be holy in himself and in the unfolding of his will. How different it is to pray that God's will be done, before we ask for daily bread! The transformation of envy for the Christian is to desire honestly and earnestly that God's will be done in the advancement of his kingdom, no matter what implications this has in the way of physical bounty. This is not a prayer of resignation, but of spiritual intensity. We need reflection to find what we yearn to see in the accomplishment of God's will among us—in his church and in all the progress of his kingdom. The spread of the gospel becomes a daily part of our intercession. In place of grumbling and complaining, we know contentment, but more—yearning to hear the name of Jesus being lifted up, and joy in the triumphs of the gospel. The Spirit dispels greed. We desire now the honor of the Savior.

COVETING OTHER THAN MATERIAL THINGS

The temptations to covetousness are subtle. Christians can fall prey to covetousness even within the fellowship of love in the church, as they advance together with other Christians in a "partnership in the gospel." In sinful selfishness, we are tempted to envy even the spiritual gifts of others who minister to us. Paul in prison felt the envy that other leaders had for him. They were glad he was in prison so that his gifts would not outshine theirs. Paul could accept this, however, knowing that Christ was being preached. Yet Paul rejoiced even more in Timothy, his son in the gospel, because Timothy's motives for kingdom work were pure. "I have no one else like him," Paul wrote, "who takes a genuine interest in your welfare. For everyone looks out for his own interests, not those of Jesus Christ" (Phil. 2:20–21).

While Jesus searches our hearts to see whether we are obedient to the tenth commandment, he also transforms it and fulfills it. We all stand before his gaze, as did Peter, hearing him ask, "Do you love me?" (John 21:15–17). I don't know about you, but I feel sorry for Peter. I understand his passion and his foolishness, having made similar claims (though perhaps not out loud!) in my own life of service. Peter bragged, "Even if all fall away, I will not" (Mark 14:29). Jesus replied, "Today—yes, tonight—before the rooster crows twice you yourself will disown me three times" (Mark 14:30). How foolish and ashamed Peter must have felt! How bitterly he must have regretted his rash words, and how much more bitterly did he regret his words of denial. From a passionate desire to further Christ's cause, he had stooped to a flat, lying denial of his Lord.

But Jesus is full of mercy. He understands our weakness and knows that we are dust. Jesus appeared individually to Simon Peter after the resurrection, then restored him as an apostle at a fish breakfast by the Lake of Galilee. Three times Jesus asked

Peter whether he loved him, and Peter replied in great distress, "Lord, you know all things; you know that I love you" (John 21:17). Swallowed by Christ's great mercy and zeal for the kingdom, Peter's abject denial was not enough to disqualify him from service. On the contrary, his understanding of grace had grown by leaps and bounds, and he was now, far better than before, prepared to speak out for the cause of Christ. Restored in Christ's love and the power of the Spirit, Peter was commissioned again to feed Christ's sheep. The heart-searching of the commandment of love restores even the disciple who blasphemed in denying Christ while Jesus stood on trial. With the widening and deepening of the commandments goes the searching and restoring of Christ's Spirit, purifying his church in that love that he commands—and gives.

At the beginning of this chapter, we noted that the sin of covetousness seems an odd sin to close out the tablets of the law. It is truly the one commandment that we cannot keep, however, for it demands that we love God with all our heart, soul, strength, and mind, and our neighbor as ourselves—with no respite, no excuse, no caveats. Paul realized that the law's demands were pervasive: "Sin, seizing an opportunity through the commandment, produced in me all kinds of covetousness" (Rom. 7:8 ESV). He understood that covetousness was ever-present in our hearts and that to obey the tenth commandment we must covet love above all things: "Covet earnestly the best gifts: and yet shew I unto you a more excellent way" (1 Cor. 12:31 KJV). Covetousness is one of the most comprehensive commands because it denies all loves but the love of God. This command brings us back to the first commandment to love the Lord with all our hearts.

I pray that as you meditate on the unrelenting demands made by God in his law, you will also be greatly comforted to know that Jesus has fulfilled all of the law's demands on your behalf and that by his Spirit he will conform you to his image as you trust in him. He will fill your heart with the ability to love him and to love others. He will finish the work he has begun in you and present you faultless before the throne of the Father, who will pronounce you pure and guiltless on his final judgment day.

STUDY QUESTIONS

Think It Through:

1. How does the tenth commandment differ from the other nine?

2. How does modern advertising stimulate envy?

3. Buddhism finds freedom in the death of desire. Does this commandment say the same thing?

4. What treasure does the Christian mind-set desire?

5. How would you summarize the way Jesus transformed the law? Apply this transformation to the Great Commandment.

Take It to Heart:

1. Pray the Lord's Prayer. Do you really desire above all that God's kingdom will come and his will be done? We seek our heart's desire. Do you seek first the King and his kingdom? Your treasure is the Lord himself. His power is your strength.

2. Reflect on the peace and joy that the Lord's presence brings. All creation speaks of him. Your life is in his calling; his blessing rests on your work. The fragrance of his grace surrounds his people in the world.

12

CONCLUSION

Christ fulfills the law, not by diminishing it, but by deepening and widening it. In every one of the Ten Commandments, we see not only the negative commands, but their positive requirements.

Having no other gods implies loving God with all our heart, soul, strength, and mind.

Not bowing to idols means honoring and revering God as Creator and Redeemer in our every thought, capturing all our thoughts to Christ.

Not misusing God's name means honoring that name in every moment of our lives, and confessing it in witness by both our words and our actions.

Remembering the Sabbath means finding our joy and rest in laboring for God and his kingdom not only one day a week, but all seven.

Honoring our parents means accepting and promoting those family values that God set into creation and honoring all God's family members.

Avoiding murder implies loving and protecting life and the image of God in man.

Avoiding adultery means keeping our hearts pure from lust and from twisting sexuality to suit our appetites. It also implies placing love for God above all other loves.

Ceasing to steal is insufficient to obey God's command, which demands that we work hard to earn enough money to be lavish and extravagant in graciously giving it away to those in need.

Not bearing false witness implies that in every situation we must honor the reputations of those around us, refusing to allow any shadow of dishonor to fall across their reputations because of our words. It also means that our words are to bear testimony to the truth of God and to the person of Christ.

Refusing to covet means that our hearts must be completely sold out to the good of the kingdom and thoroughly careless about the material implications of that passion.

How impossible to keep the commandments! The law is cited in the Epistles as the law "in the Lord" (Eph. 6:1). One day, we will all stand before the bench—not of a judge with the Ten Commandments posted on a wall behind him, but of the Author of those commandments. Praise God that the Ten Commandments not only have been intensified by Christ, but also have been transformed and fulfilled in his righteousness. The law is transformed in the full measure of the love of Christ. The love that fulfills the law is the love by which Christ gave himself to redeem those given him by the Father, and by which the Father gave his one and only Son.

As we live by the Spirit who raised Jesus from the dead, we can do what the law had no power to help us accomplish.

> "For what the law was powerless to do in that it was weakened by the sinful nature, God did by sending his own Son in the likeness of sinful man to be a sin offering. And so he condemned sin in sinful man, in order that the righteous requirements of the law might be fully met in us, who do not live according to the sinful nature but according to the Spirit." (Rom. 8:3–4)

Christian, take heart. Christ has accomplished the law for you, and it is in the confidence and the freedom that Christ brings you that you can, by the power of his Spirit, please God and live out in your own life what the will of God demands of you. You will not do this perfectly. But you need not do it perfectly because God has looked on Christ and pardoned you. So reflect on all that Christ has done for you in perfectly keeping each of God's commandments, and go out today rejoicing, ready to do the work that God has prepared in advance for you, knowing that you have already been prepared for that work. As you close the covers of this book, reflect on the work of the Great High Priest who pleads your cause in the heavenly courts, sparing you from the condemnation of the law and providing you with supernatural grace and power to live the law of Christ's love:

> Before the throne of God above,
> I have a strong and perfect plea,
> A great High Priest whose name is "Love,"
> Who ever lives and pleads for me.
> My name is graven on his hands,
> My name is written on his heart;
> I know that while in heav'n he stands
> No tongue can bid me thence depart.
>
> When Satan tempts me to despair,
> And tells me of the guilt within,
> Upward I look and see him there
> Who made an end of all my sin.
> Because the sinless Savior died,
> My sinful soul is counted free;
> For God the just is satisfied
> To look on him and pardon me.

Behold him there! the risen Lamb,
My perfect, spotless Righteousness,
The great unchangeable I AM,
The King of glory and of grace!
One with himself I cannot die,
My soul is purchased by his blood;
My life is hid with Christ on high,
With Christ my Savior and my God.

Charite Lees Bancroft

NOTES

Preface

1. *Westminster Confession of Faith, Together with the Larger Catechism and the Shorter Catechism* (Atlanta: CE&P, Presbyterian Church in America, 1990), questions 42 and 105.

Chapter One: The Covenant Lord Fulfills the Law

1. See Isaiah 54:10–12; 66:12; and Jeremiah 33:15–16, to name just a few.

2. See Vern Poythress, *The Shadow of Christ in the Law of Moses* (Brentwood, TN: Wolgemuth & Hyatt, 1991), especially his section on the meaning of *fulfill* in this passage, chap. 17, pp. 251ff., and app. C, pp. 363ff.

Chapter Two: The First Commandment

1. See also Luke 9:35; John 8:40.

2. The term *Son of Man* does not so much emphasize Jesus' humanity as his authority, as can be seen in its Old Testament use.

Chapter Three: The Second Commandment

1. Title of Francis Schaeffer's well-known book *The God Who Is There* (Downer's Grove, IL: IVP, 1968).

2. See Rick Weiss, "Of Mice, Men and In-Between: Scientists Debate Blending of Human, Animal Forms," *Washington Post*, November 20, 2004.

3. [Ed. Probably a reference to Bruce Marchiano's depiction of Jesus in the film *Matthew*, the first film of the Visual Bible, produced by Visual International Ltd.]

4. Shaye I. D. Cohen: Professor of Judaic Studies, and Samuel Ungerleider, Professor of Religious Studies, Brown University. See http://www.pbs.org/wgbh/pages/frontline/shows/religion/jesus/searching.html.

5. Excerpt from John Shelby Spong, "Who Is Christ for Us?" chap. 14 in *Rescuing the Bible from Fundamentalism* (San Francisco: HarperSanFrancisco, 1992). See http://www.escapefromwatchtower.com/spong3.html.

Chapter Four: The Third Commandment

1. See Leviticus 19:12.
2. Leviticus 18:21.
3. See 2 Chronicles 33:4–7.
4. The Westminster Confession has a chapter, "Of Lawful Oaths and Vows," defending limited uses of lawful oaths. The argument is based on Jesus' acceptance of the oath required of him in his trial before the Sanhedrin (Matt. 26:63ff.), and on Paul's taking of an oath about his own intentions toward the Corinthians (2 Cor. 1:23).
5. Hymn by David Clowney, "God, All Nature Sings Thy Glory," *Trinity Hymnal* (Suwanee, GA: Great Commission Publications, 1990), No. 122.
6. Ibid.

Chapter Five: The Fourth Commandment

1. Jesus' words remind us of the creation, when God finishes his work and enters the Sabbath rest. It is fitting that the seventh-day rest becomes a first-day celebration of Christ's accomplished work and his resurrection triumph on the first day of the week.
2. On the issue of circumcision, however, Paul insisted that the change be maintained. Here the New Covenant itself was at stake.

Chapter Six: The Fifth Commandment

1. It is mistaken to suppose that "submit to one another" means that everyone submits to everyone in an egalitarian sense. Paul goes on to explain just how these patterns of submission work out.

Chapter Seven: The Sixth Commandment

1. Richard Miniter, "The Dutch Way of Death," *Wall Street Journal*, April 25, 2001.

2. Ibid. The cited article describes a Dr. Nico Wolswinkel, who could not bring himself to kill a 77-year-old woman dying of cancer, at her request. "He couldn't bring himself to kill his patient; doctors are supposed to be healers, not killers. And, as a Christian, he believed it was wrong to take into his hands the power of God. A few days later, his patient died naturally."

3. Francis Steen, "Peter Singer: Ethics in the Age of Evolutionary Psychology," *The Philosopher's Magazine*, March 7, 2000 (http://cog web.ucla.edu/Debate/SingerPM.html). Steen is reporting on an interview with Singer after a debate at the University of California, Santa Barbara, March 7, 2000. See Helga Kuhse & Peter Singer, *Should the Baby Live? The Problem of Handicapped Infants* (New York: Oxford University Press, 1985); *Animal Liberation*, 2nd ed. (New York: New York Review of Books, 1990).

4. Vern Poythress, *The Shadow of Christ in the Law of Moses* (Brentwood, TN: Wolgemuth & Hyatt, 1991), 159–63.

Chapter Eight: The Seventh Commandment

1. *The Sacramento Bee*, January 13, 2005.

2. The translation "be silent" follows the Hebrew, as in the ASV margin.

3. Robert Spitzer, M.D., Professor of Psychiatry, Columbia University, "Psychiatry and Homosexuality," *Wall Street Journal*, May 23, 2001.

4. George Croly, "Spirit of God, Descend upon My Heart," *Trinity Hymnal* (Suwanee, GA: Great Commission Publications, 1990), No. 338.

Chapter Nine: The Eighth Commandment

1. http://www.latimes.com/news/local/la-fires-08-pulitzer,1,7817 335.story?coll=la-adelphia-right-rail&ctrack=2&cset=true.

2. In recognizing the solidity of our inheritance, Peter is realistic. He speaks of sufferings to come. Faith must endure all kinds of trials. "These

have come so that your faith—of greater worth than gold, which perishes even though refined by fire—may be proved genuine and may result in praise, glory and honor when Jesus Christ is revealed" (1 Peter 1:7).

Chapter Ten: The Ninth Commandment

1. [Ed. This phrase refers to a collection of essays by C. S. Lewis, *God in the Dock: Essays on Theology and Ethics* (USA, Trustees of the Estate of C. S. Lewis, 1970).]

2. John Frame's lectures were distributed to an adult class at New Life Presbyterian Church of Escondido, California: "What God Wants Us to Believe and Do, II. Westminster Shorter Catechism, Questions 39–107."

3. From the title of Francis Schaeffer's work *The Church before the Watching World: A Practical Ecclesiolgy* (Downer's Grove, IL: IVP, 1971).

Chapter Eleven: The Tenth Commandment

1. Professor Frame, now of Reformed Theological Seminary in Orlando, Florida, recommends Herbert Schlossberg, *Idols for Destruction: The Conflict of Christian Faith and American Culture* (Wheaton, IL: Crossway, 1990), as an "excellent account of the dynamics of envy in world history. Critique of socialism as based on envy of the rich and successful."

2. See http://abclocal.go.com/wls/story?section=news&id=2602774.

INDEX OF SCRIPTURE

Born in Philadelphia on July 30, 1917, **Edmund P. Clowney** received his BA from Wheaton College, a Th.B from Westminster Theological Seminary, an STM from Yale University Divinity School, and a DD from Wheaton College. Ed taught practical theology at Westminster Theological Seminary in Philadelphia from 1952 to 1984, serving as its president for sixteen of those years. From 1984 to 1990 and again from 2002 to 2005, he served as theologian-in-residence at Trinity Presbyterian Church in Charlottesville, Virginia. Between these two periods, he spent twelve years teaching at Westminster Seminary in Escondido, California, then two years as associate pastor of Christ the King Presbyterian Church in Houston, Texas.

He and his wife, Jean, who is still living in Charlottesville, were married for sixty-three years and have five children, twenty-one grandchildren, and sixteen great-grandchildren. Ed was known for his humble and gentle spirit, his fair-mindedness, his passion for seeing and preaching Christ from all the Scriptures, his visionary creativity for Kingdom work, his enthusiasm for children's ministries, and his dry humor. For more information on Ed's life, please visit www.edmundclowney.com.

Rebecca Clowney Jones, daughter of Dr. and Mrs. Clowney, is married to Dr. Peter Jones, with whom she served as a missionary in France for eighteen years. She now acts as editor and part-time secretary for her husband, who is the director of Christian Witness to a Pagan Planet. Rebecca has taught Graduate Writing Skills at Westminster Seminary California and presently serves on the board of the Council for Biblical Manhood and Womanhood. She is an active member of Women in the Church in her denomination (PCA) and speaks for women's retreats and conferences. She and Peter have seven children and ten grandchildren.